The Erosion of Civilian Control of the Military in the United States Today

Richard H. Kohn

Dr. Kohn is professor of history and chairman of the Curriculum in Peace, War, and Defense at the University of North Carolina at Chapel Hill. After undergraduate study at Harvard and earning a doctorate at the University of Wisconsin, he taught at City College, City University of New York; Rutgers University–New Brunswick; and at the National and U.S. Army War Colleges. He served as chief of Air Force history and chief historian of the U.S. Air Force, 1981–1991. Most recently he edited (with Peter Feaver) Soldiers and Civilians: The Civil-Military Gap and American National Security (2001), reviewed in this issue.

This article is an expansion and update of the Harmon Memorial Lecture in Military History delivered in December 1999 at the U.S. Air Force Academy. Earlier versions were given as lectures at the Army, Air, Naval, Marine Corps, and National War Colleges, the Marine Corps and Air Command and Staff Colleges, the U.S. Military Academy, U.S. Central Command, the Duke University Law School national security law course, the Syracuse University national security management course, the University of North Carolina at Pembroke, and, at the invitation of the Chairman, the Joint Staff.

The author thanks Andrew J. Bacevich, George A. Billias, Eliot A. Cohen, Peter D. Feaver, Thomas C. Greenwood, Paul Herbert, Peter Karsten, Lynne H. Kohn, and Abigail A. Kohn for criticisms and suggestions, and numerous other friends, colleagues, and officers and civilians in audiences who offered questions and comments. Jonathan Phillips, Erik Riker-Coleman, and Michael Allsep provided indispensable research assistance.

© 2002 by Richard H. Kohn
Naval War College Review, Summer 2002, Vol. LV, No. 3

THE EROSION OF CIVILIAN CONTROL OF THE MILITARY IN THE UNITED STATES TODAY

Richard H. Kohn

I n over thirty-five years as a military historian, I have come to have great re-spect for and trust in American military officers. The United States is truly blessed to have men and women of the highest character leading its youth and safeguarding its security. That fact makes the present subject all the more trou-bling and unpleasant, whether to write or read about it. However, the subject is crucial to the nation's security and to its survival as a republic. I am speaking of a tear in the nation's civil and political fabric; my hope is that by bringing it to the attention of a wide military and defense readership I can prompt a frank, open discussion that could, by raising the awareness of the American public and alert-ing the armed forces, set in motion a process of healing.

My subject is the civil-military relationship at the pinnacle of the govern-ment, and my fear, baldly stated, is that in recent years civilian control of the military has weakened in the United States and is threatened today. The issue is not the nightmare of a coup d'état but rather the evidence that the Ameri-can military has grown in influence to the point of being able to impose its own perspective on many policies and decisions. What I have detected is no conspiracy but repeated efforts on the part of the armed forces to frustrate or evade civilian authority when that opposition seems likely to preclude out-comes the military dislikes.

While I do not see any crisis, I am convinced that civilian control has dimin-ished to the point where it could alter the character of American government and undermine national defense. My views result from nearly four decades of reading and reflection about civilian control in this country; from personal ob-servation from inside the Pentagon during the 1980s; and since then, from watching the Clinton and two Bush administrations struggle to balance national security with domestic political realities.

Understanding the problem begins with a review of the state of civil-military relations during the last nine years, a state of affairs that in my judgment has been extraordinarily poor, in many respects as low as in any period of American peacetime history. No president was ever as reviled by the professional military—treated with such disrespect, or viewed with such contempt—as Bill Clinton. Conversely, no administration ever treated the military with more fear and deference on the one hand, and indifference and neglect on the other, as the Clinton administration.

The relationship began on a sour note during the 1992 campaign. As a youth, Clinton had avoided the draft, written a letter expressing "loathing" for the military, and demonstrated against the Vietnam War while in Britain on a Rhodes scholarship. Relations turned venomous with the awful controversy over gays in the military, when the administration—in ignorance and arrogance—announced its intention to abolish the ban on open homosexual service immediately, without study or consultation. The Joint Chiefs of Staff responded by resisting, floating rumors of their own and dozens of other resignations, encouraging their retired brethren to arouse congressional and public opposition, and then more or less openly negotiating a compromise with their commander in chief.[1]

The newly elected president was publicly insulted by service people (including a two-star general) in person, in print, and in speeches. So ugly was the behavior that commanders had to remind their subordinates of their constitutional and legal obligations not to speak derogatorily of the civilian leadership; the Air Force chief of staff felt obliged to remind his senior commanders "about core values, including the principle of a chain of command that runs from the president right down to our newest airman."[2]

Nothing like this had ever occurred in American history. This was the most open manifestation of defiance and resistance by the American military since the publication of the Newburgh addresses over two centuries earlier, at the close of the American war for independence. Then the officers of the Army openly contemplated revolt or resignation en masse over the failure of Congress to pay them or to fund the pensions they had been promised during a long and debilitating war. All of this led me, as a student of American civil-military relations, to ask why so loyal, subordinate, and successful a military, as professional as any in the world, suddenly violated one of its most sacred traditions.

While open conflict soon dropped from public sight, bitterness hardened into a visceral hatred that became part of the culture of many parts of the military establishment, kept alive by a continuous stream of incidents and controversies.[3] These included, to cite but a few: the undermining and driving from office of Secretary of Defense Les Aspin in 1993, followed by the humiliating withdrawal of his nominated replacement; controversies over the retirements of at least six four-star flag officers, including the early retirement of an Air Force chief of staff (an unprecedented occurrence); and the tragic suicide of a Chief of Naval Operations (also unprecedented). There were ceaseless arguments over gender, the most continuous source of conflict between the Clinton administration and its na-

William J. Clinton
(White House)

tional security critics.[4] The specific episodes ranged from the botched investigations of the 1991 Tailhook scandal to the 1997 uproar over Air Force first lieutenant Kelly Flinn, the first female B-52 line pilot, who (despite admitting to adultery, lying to an investigating officer, and disobeying orders) was allowed to leave the service without court-martial. Other related incidents included the outrages at Aberdeen Proving Ground, where Army sergeants had sex with recruits under their command, and the 1999 retirement of the highest-ranking female Army general in history amid accusations that she had been sexually harassed by a fellow general officer some years previously. In addition, there were bitter arguments over readiness; over budgets; over whether and how to intervene with American forces abroad, from Somalia to Haiti to Bosnia to Kosovo; and over national strategy generally.[5]

So poisonous became the relationship that two Marine officers in 1998 had to be reprimanded for violating article 88 of the Uniform Code of Military Justice, the provision about contemptuous words against the highest civilian officials. The assistant commandant of the Marine Corps felt constrained to warn all Marine generals about officers publicly criticizing or disparaging the commander in chief.[6] The next year, at a military ball at the Plaza Hotel in New York City, a local television news anchor, playing on the evening's theme, "A Return to Integrity," remarked that he "didn't recognize any dearth of integrity here" until he "realized that President Clinton was in town"—and the crowd, "which included 20 generals" and was made up largely of officers, went wild.[7] During the election of 2000, the chief legal officers of two of the largest commands in the Army and Air Force issued warnings lest resentment over Gore campaign challenges to absentee ballots in Florida boil over into open contempt.[8]

These illustrations emphasize the negatives. In contrast, by all accounts people in uniform respected and worked well with Secretary of Defense William Perry. Certainly Generals John Shalikashvili and Hugh Shelton, successive chairmen of the Joint Chiefs of Staff after 1993, appeared to have been liked and respected by civilians in the Clinton administration. But these men, and other senior officers and officials who bridged the two cultures at the top levels of government, seemed to understand that theirs was a delicate role—to mediate between two hostile relatives who feared and distrusted each other but realized that they had to work together if both were to survive.

Now, to discount the Clinton difficulties as atmospherics and thus essentially insignificant would be mistaken, for the toxicity of the civil-military relationship damaged national security in at least three ways: first, by paralyzing national security policy; second, by obstructing and in some cases sabotaging American ability to intervene in foreign crises or to exercise leadership internationally; and third, by undermining the confidence of the armed forces in their own uniformed leadership.

In response to that first, searing controversy over open homosexual service, the administration concluded that this president—with his Democratic affiliation, liberal leanings, history of draft evasion and opposition to the Vietnam War, and admitted marital infidelity and experimentation with marijuana—would never be acceptable to the military.[9] One knowledgeable insider characterized the White House of those years as reflecting the demography of the post-Vietnam Democratic Party—people who had never served in uniform and who had a "tin ear" for things military. Knowing little or nothing about military affairs or national security and not caring to develop a deep or sympathetic understanding of either, the administration decided that for this president, military matters constituted a "third rail."[10] No issue with the military was worth exposing this vulnerability; nothing was worth the cost. All controversy with the military was therefore to be avoided. In fact, the Clintonites from the beginning tried to "give away" the military establishment: first to the congressional Democrats, by making Les Aspin secretary of defense; then, when Aspin was driven from office, to the military itself, by nominating Admiral Bobby Inman; then, when he withdrew, to the military-industrial complex (with William Perry as secretary and John Deutsch and John White as deputies), an arrangement that lasted until 1997; and finally to the Republicans, in the person of Senator William Cohen of Maine. From the outset, the focus of the administration in foreign affairs was almost wholly economic in nature, and while that may have been genius, one result of the Clintonites' inattention and inconstancy was the disgust and disrespect of the national security community, particularly those in uniform.[11] By the time Clinton left office, some officials were admitting that he had been "unwilling to exercise full authority over military commanders."[12] "Those who monitored Clinton closely during his eight years as president believed . . . that he was intimidated more by the military than by any other political force he dealt with," reported David Halberstam. Said "a former senior N[ational]

S[ecurity] C[ouncil] official who studied [Clinton] closely, . . . 'he was out-and-out afraid of them.'"[13]

Forging a reasonable and economical national security policy was crucial to the health and well-being of the country, particularly at a time of epochal transition brought on by the end of the Cold War. But both the first Bush and then Clinton's administration studiously avoided any public discussion of what role the United States should play in the world, unless asserting the existence of a "new world order" or labeling the United States "the indispensable nation" constitutes discussion.[14] As for the Clinton administration, indifference to military affairs and the decision to take no risks and expend no political capital in that area produced paralysis. Any rethinking of strategy, force structure, roles and missions of the armed services, organization, personnel, weapons, or other choices indispensable for the near and long term was rendered futile. As a result, today, over a decade after the end of the Cold War, there is still no common understanding about the fundamental purposes of the American military establishment or the principles by which the United States will decide whether to use military power in pursuit of the national interest.

The Clinton administration held itself hostage to the organization and force structure of the Cold War.[15] At the beginning of Clinton's first term, Secretary Aspin attempted to modify the basis of American strategy—an ability to fight two "major regional contingencies" (changed later to "major theater wars") almost simultaneously. But Aspin caved in to charges that such a change would

Colin Powell (IRI).

embolden America's adversaries and weaken security arrangements with allies in the Middle East and Asia.[16] The result was a defense budget known to be inadequate for the size and configuration of the military establishment even without the need to fund peacetime intervention contingencies, which constantly threw military accounts into deficit.[17] Budgets became prisoners of readiness. Forces could not be reduced, because of the many military commitments around the world, but if readiness to wage high-intensity combat fell or seemed to diminish, Republican critics would rise up in outrage. Thus the uniformed leadership—each service chief, regional or functional commander, sometimes even division, task force, or wing commanders—possessed the political weight to veto any significant change in the nation's fundamental security structure.

As a result, the Clinton administration never could match resources with commitments, balance readiness with modernization, or consider organizational changes that would relieve the stresses on personnel and equipment.[18] All of this occurred when the services were on the brink of, or were actually undergoing, what many believed to be changes in weaponry and tactics so major as to constitute a "revolution in military affairs."[19] One consequence of the insufficiency of resources in people and money to meet frequent operational commitments and growing maintenance costs was the loss of many of the best officers and noncommissioned officers, just as economic prosperity and other factors were reducing the numbers of men and women willing to sign up for military service in the first place.

The paralysis in military policy in the 1990s provoked the Congress to attempt by legislation at least four different times to force the Pentagon to reevaluate national security policy, strategy, and force structure, with as yet no significant result.[20] Perhaps the last of these efforts, the U.S. Commission on National Security/21st Century (also called the Hart-Rudman Commission), which undertook a comprehensive review of national security and the military establishment, will have some effect. If so, it will be because the Bush administration possessed the political courage to brave the civil-military friction required to reorganize an essentially Cold War military establishment into a force capable of meeting the security challenges of the twenty-first century.[21] But the prospects are not encouraging when one considers Secretary of Defense Donald

Donald Rumsfeld
(Defenselink)

Rumsfeld's secrecy and lack of consultation with the uniformed military and Congress; the forces gathering to resist change; the priority of the Bush tax cut and national missile defense, which threaten to limit severely the money available and to force excruciating choices; and Rumsfeld's fudging of the very concept of "transformation." Even the 11 September 2001 terrorist attacks have not broken the logjam, except perhaps monetarily. The administration has committed itself to slow, incremental change so as not to confront the inherent conservatism of the armed services or imperil the weapons purchases pushed so powerfully by defense contractors and their congressional champions.[22] The White House has done so despite its belief that the failure to exert civilian control in the 1990s left a military establishment declining in quality and effectiveness.

Second, the Clinton administration—despite far more frequent occasions for foreign armed intervention (which was ironic, considering its aversion to military matters)—was often immobilized over when, where, how, and under what circumstances to use military force in the world. The long, agonizing debates and vacillation over intervention in Africa, Haiti, and the former Yugoslavia reflected in part the weakness of the administration compared to the political power of the uniformed military.[23] The lack of trust between the two sides distorted decision making to an extreme. Sometimes the military exercised a veto over the use of American force, or at least an ability so to shape the character of American intervention that means determined ends—a roundabout way of exercising a veto. At other times, civilians ignored or even avoided receiving advice from the military. By the 1999 Kosovo air campaign, the consultative relationship had so broken down that the president was virtually divorced from his theater commander, and that commander's communications with the secretary of defense and chairman of the Joint Chiefs were corrupted by misunderstanding and distrust. The result was a campaign misconceived at the outset and badly coordinated not only between civilian and military but between the various levels of command. The consequences could have undone the Nato alliance, and they certainly stiffened Serbian will, exacerbated divisions within Nato councils, increased criticism in the United States, and prolonged the campaign beyond what almost everyone involved had predicted.[24]

Last, the incessant acrimony—the venomous atmosphere in Washington—shook the confidence of the armed forces in their own leadership. Different groups accused the generals and admirals, at one extreme, of caving in to political correctness, and at the other, of being rigid and hidebound with respect to gender integration, war-fighting strategy, and organizational change. The impact on morale contributed to the hemorrhage from the profession of arms of able young and middle-rank officers. The loss of so many fine officers, combined with declines in recruiting (which probably brought, in turn, a diminution in the quality of new officers and enlisted recruits), may weaken the nation's military leadership in the next generation and beyond, posing greater danger to national security than would any policy blunder. Certainly many complex factors have driven people out of uniform and impaired recruiting, but the loss of confidence in the senior uniformed leadership has been cited by many as a reason to leave the service.[25]

Now, to attribute all of these difficulties to the idiosyncrasies of the Clinton administration alone would be a mistake. In fact, the recent friction in civil-military relations and unwillingness to exert civilian control have roots all the way back to World War II. Unquestionably Mr. Clinton and his appointees bungled civil-military relations badly, from the beginning. But other administrations have done so also, and others will in the future.

If one measures civilian control not by the superficial standard of who signs the papers and passes the laws but by the relative influence of the uniformed military and civilian policy makers in the two great areas of concern in military affairs—national security policy, and the use of force to protect the country and project power abroad—then civilian control has deteriorated significantly in the last generation. In theory, civilians have the authority to issue virtually any order and organize the military in any fashion they choose. But in practice, the relationship is far more complex. Both sides frequently disagree among themselves. Further, the military can evade or circumscribe civilian authority by framing the alternatives or tailoring their advice or predicting nasty consequences; by leaking information or appealing to public opinion (through various indirect channels, like lobbying groups or retired generals and admirals); or by approaching friends in the Congress for support. They can even fail to implement decisions, or carry them out in such a way as to stymie their intent. The reality is that civilian control is not a fact but a process, measured across a spectrum—something *situational*, dependent on the people, issues, and the political and military forces involved. We are not talking about a coup here, or anything else demonstrably illegal; we are talking about who calls the tune in military affairs in the United States today.[26]

Contrast the weakness of the civilian side with the strength of the military, not only in the policy process but in clarity of definition of American purpose, consistency of voice, and willingness to exert influence both in public and behind the scenes.

The power of the military within the policy process has been growing steadily since a low point under Secretary of Defense Robert McNamara in the 1960s. Under the 1986 Goldwater-Nichols Defense Reorganization Act, the chairman of the Joint Chiefs of Staff (JCS) has influence that surpasses that of everyone else within the Pentagon except the secretary of defense, and the chairman possesses a more competent, focused, and effective staff than the secretary does, as well as, often, a clearer set of goals, fewer political constraints, and under some circumstances greater credibility with the public.[27] In the glow of success in the Gulf War, efforts to exorcise Vietnam, the high public esteem now enjoyed by the armed forces, and the disgust Americans have felt for politics in general and for partisanship in particular, the stature of the chairman has grown to a magnitude out of proportion to his legal or institutional position.

The Joint Staff is the most powerful organization in the Department of Defense; frequently, by dint of its speed, agility, knowledge, and expertise, the Joint Staff frames the choices.[28] The Joint Requirements Oversight Council (the vice chiefs, convening under the vice chairman to prioritize joint programs in terms of need and cost) has gathered influence and authority over the most basic issues of weapons and force structure.[29] Within the bureaucracy, JCS has a representative in the interagency decision process, giving the uniformed military a voice separate from that of the Department of Defense. Similarly, the armed services maintain their own congressional liaison and public affairs offices, bureaucracies so large that they are impossible to monitor fully. (One officer admitted to me privately that his duty on Capitol Hill was to encourage Congress to restore a billion dollars that the Pentagon's civilian leadership had cut out of his service's budget request.)[30] Moreover, the regional commanders have come to assume such importance in their areas—particularly in the Pacific, the Middle East, and Central Asia—that they have effectively displaced American ambassadors and the State Department as the primary instruments of American foreign policy.[31] In recent reorganizations, these commanders have so increased in stature and influence within the defense establishment that their testimony can sway Congress and embarrass or impede the administration, especially when the civilians in the executive branch are weak and the Congress is dominated by an aggressively led opposition political party.

One knowledgeable commentator put it this way in early 1999: "The dirty little secret of American civil-military relations, by no means unique to this [the Clinton] administration, is that the commander in chief does not command the military establishment; he cajoles it, negotiates with it, and, as necessary, appeases it."[32] A high Pentagon civilian privately substantiates the interpretation: what "weighs heavily . . . every day" is "the reluctance, indeed refusal, of the political appointees to disagree with the military on any matter, not just operational matters." In fact, so powerful have such institutional forces become, and so intractable the problem of altering the military establishment, that the new Rumsfeld regime in the Pentagon decided to conduct its comprehensive review of national defense in strict secrecy, effectively cutting the regional commanders, the service chiefs, and the Congress out of the process so that resistance could not organize in advance of the intended effort at transformation.[33]

Furthermore, senior military leaders have been able to use their personal leverage for a variety of purposes, sometimes because of civilian indifference, or deference, or ignorance, sometimes because they have felt it necessary to fill voids of policy and decision making. But sometimes the influence is exercised intentionally and purposefully, even aggressively. After fifty years of cold war, the "leak," the bureaucratic maneuver, the alliance with partisans in Congress—the *ménage à trois* between the administration, Congress, and the military—have become a way of life, in which services and groups employ their knowledge, contacts, and positions to promote personal or institutional agendas.[34] In the 1970s, responding to the view widely held among military officers that a reserve callup would have galvanized public support for Vietnam, allowed intensified prosecution of the war, and prevented divorce between the Army and the American people, the Army chief of staff deliberately redesigned divisions to contain "round-out" units of reserve or National Guard troops, making it impossible for the president to commit the Army to battle on a large scale without mobilizing the reserves and Guard.[35] In the 1980s, the chairman of the Joint Chiefs, Admiral William J. Crowe, worked "behind the scenes" to encourage Congress to strengthen his own office even though the secretary of defense opposed such a move. During the Iran-Iraq War Crowe pushed for American escort of Kuwaiti tankers in the Persian Gulf, because he believed it important for American foreign policy. He and the chiefs strove to slow the Reagan administration's strategic missile defense program. Crowe even went so far as to create a personal communications channel with his Soviet military counterpart, apparently unknown to his civilian superiors, to avert any possibility of a misunderstanding leading to war. "It was in the nature of the Chairman's job," Crowe

William J. Crowe
Naval Institute, Annapolis, Md.

remembered, "that I occasionally found myself fighting against Defense Department positions as well as for them."[36]

In the 1990s, press leaks from military sources led directly to the weakening and ultimate dismissal of the Clinton administration's first secretary of defense.[37] In 1994 the Chief of Naval Operations (CNO) openly discussed with senior commanders his plans to manipulate the Navy budget and operations tempo to force his preferred priorities on the Office of the Secretary of Defense and Congress. When a memo recounting the conversation surfaced in the press, no civilian in authority called the CNO to account.[38] The 1995 Commission on the Roles and Missions of the Armed Forces recommended consolidating the staffs of the service chiefs and the service secretaries; no one mentioned the diminution of civilian control that would have taken place as a result.[39]

Even during the 1990s, a period when the administration appeared to be forceful, insisting upon the use of American forces over military objections or resistance, the uniformed leadership often arbitrated events. The 1995 Bosnia intervention was something of a paradigm. American priorities seem to have been, first, deploying in overwhelming strength, in order to suffer few if any casualties; second, establishing a deadline for exit; third, issuing "robust" rules of engagement, again to forestall casualties; fourth, narrowing the definition of the mission to ensure that it was incontrovertibly "doable"; and fifth—*fifth*—reconstructing Bosnia as a viable independent country.[40]

In recent years senior uniformed leaders have spoken out on issues of policy—undoubtedly often with the encouragement or at least the acquiescence of civilian officials, but not always so. Sometimes these pronouncements endeavor to sell policies and decisions to the public or within the government before a presidential decision, even though such advocacy politicizes the chairman, a chief, or a regional commander and inflates their influence in discussions of policy. A four-star general, a scant ten days after retiring, publishes a long article in our most respected foreign affairs journal, preceded by a *New York Times* op-ed piece. In them, he criticizes the administration's most sensitive (and vulnerable) policy—and virtually no one in the press or elsewhere questions whether his action was professionally appropriate.[41] The chairman of the Joint Chiefs of Staff gives "an impassioned interview" to the *New York Times* "on the folly of intervention" in Bosnia as "the first Bush administration" is pondering "the question of whether to intervene."[42] Another chairman coins the "Dover Principle," cautioning the civilian leadership about the human and political costs of casualties when American forces are sent into some crisis or conflict (and service members' bodies return through the joint mortuary at Dover Air Force Base). This lecture clearly aimed to establish boundaries in the public's mind and to constrain civilian freedom of action in intervening overseas.

Certainly Generals Shalikashvili and Shelton have been fairly circumspect about speaking out on issues of policy, and the current chairman, Air Force general Richard B. Myers, even more. However, their predecessor, Colin Powell, possessed and used extraordinary power throughout his tenure as chairman of the JCS. He conceived and then sold to a skeptical secretary of defense and a divided Congress the "Base Force" reorganization and reduction in 1990–91. He shaped the U.S. prosecution of the Gulf War to ensure limited objectives, the use of overwhelming force, a speedy end to combat, and the immediate exit of American forces. He spoke frequently on matters of policy during and after the election of 1992—an op-ed in the *New York Times* and a more comprehensive statement of foreign policy in the quarterly *Foreign Affairs*. Powell essentially vetoed intervention in Somalia and Bosnia, ignored or circumvented the chiefs on a regular basis, and managed the advisory process so as to present only single alternatives to civilian policy makers. All of this antedated his forcing President Clinton in 1993 to back down on allowing homosexuals to serve openly.[43] In fact, General Powell became so powerful and so adept in the bureaucratic manipulations that often decide crucial questions before the final decision maker affixes a signature that in 2001 the Bush administration installed an experienced, powerful, highly respected figure at the Defense Department specifically lest Powell control the entire foreign and national security apparatus in the new administration.[44]

All of these are examples—and only public manifestations—of a policy and decision-making process that has tilted far more toward the military than ever before in American history in peacetime.

Now an essential question arises: do these developments differ from previous practice or experience in American history? At first glance, the answer might seem to be no. Military and civilian have often differed, and the military has for many years acted on occasion beyond what might be thought proper in a republican system of government, a system that defines civilian control, or military subordination to civil authority, as obligatory.

Historical examples abound. Leading generals and chiefs of staff of the Army from James Wilkinson in the 1790s through Maxwell Taylor in the 1950s have fought with presidents and secretaries of war or defense in the open and in private over all sorts of issues—including key military policies in times of crisis. Officers openly disparaged Abraham Lincoln during the Civil War; that president's problems with his generals became legendary.[45] Two commanding generals of the Army were so antagonistic toward the War Department that they moved their headquarters out of Washington: Winfield Scott to New York in the 1850s, and William Tecumseh Sherman to St. Louis in the 1870s.[46] In the 1880s, reform-minded naval officers connived to modernize the Navy from wood and sail to steel and steam. To do so they drew the civilian leadership into the process, forged an alliance with the steel industry, and (for the first time in American history, and in coordination with political and economic elites) sold naval reform and a peacetime buildup of standing forces to the public through publications, presentations, displays, reviews, and other precursors of the promotional public relations that would be used so frequently—and effectively—in the twentieth century.[47] In the 1920s and 1930s, the youthful Army Air Corps became so adept at public relations and at generating controversy over airpower that three different presidential administrations were forced to appoint high-level boards of outsiders to study how the Army could (or could not) properly incorporate aviation.[48]

Both Presidents Roosevelt complained bitterly about the resistance of the armed services to change. "You should go through the experience of trying to get any changes in the thinking . . . and action of the career diplomats and then you'd know what a real problem was," FDR complained in 1940. "But the Treasury and the State Department put together are nothing as compared with the Na-a-vy. . . . To change anything in the Na-a-vy is like punching a feather bed. You punch it with your right and you punch it with your left until you are finally exhausted, and then you find the damn bed just as it was before you started punching."[49]

The interservice battles of the 1940s and 1950s were so fierce that neither Congress nor the president could contain them. Internecine warfare blocked President Harry Truman's effort to unify the armed forces in the 1940s ("unification" finally produced only loose confederation) and angered President Dwight D. Eisenhower through the 1950s. Neither administration fully controlled strategy, force structure, or weapons procurement; both had to fight service parochialism and interests; and both ruled largely by imposing top-line budget limits and forcing the services to struggle over a limited funding "pie." Eisenhower replaced or threatened to fire several of his chiefs. Only through Byzantine maneuvers, managerial wizardry, and draconian measures did Robert

McNamara bring a modicum of coherence and integration to the overall administration of the Defense Department in the 1960s. The price, however, was a ruthless, relentless bureaucratic struggle that not only contributed to the disaster of Vietnam but left a legacy of suspicion and deceit that infects American civil-military relations to this day.[50] (Even today, embittered officers identify their nemesis by his full name—Robert Strange McNamara—to express their loathing.) The point of this history is that civil-military relations *are* messy and frequently antagonistic; military people *do* on occasion defy civilians; civilian control *is* situational.[51]

Robert S. McNamara
(LBJ Library and Museum)

But the present differs from the past in four crucial ways.

First, the military has now largely *united* to shape, oppose, evade, or thwart civilian choices, whereas in the past the armed services were usually divided internally or among themselves. Indeed, most civil-military conflict during the Cold War arose from rivalry between the services, and over roles, missions, budgets, or new weapons systems—not whether and how to use American armed forces, or general military policy.

Second, many of the *issues* in play today reach far beyond the narrowly military, not only to the wider realm of national security but often to foreign relations more broadly. In certain cases military affairs even affect the character and values of American society itself.

Third, the role of military leaders has drifted over the last generation from that primarily of advisers and advocates within the private confines of the executive branch to a much more *public* function. As we have noted, they champion not just their services but policies and decisions in and beyond the military realm, and sometimes they mobilize public or congressional opinion either directly or indirectly (whether in Congress or the executive branch) prior to decision by civilian officials. To give but three examples: senior officers spoke out publicly on whether the United States should sign a treaty banning the use of land mines; on whether American forces should be put into the Balkans to stop ethnic cleansing; and on whether the nation should support the establishment of the International Criminal Court. Again, such actions are not unprecedented, but they have occurred recently with increasing frequency, and collectively they represent a significant encroachment on civilian control of the military.[52]

Fourth, senior officers now lead a *permanent* peacetime military establishment that differs fundamentally from any of its predecessors. Unlike the large citizen forces raised in wartime and during the Cold War, today's armed services are professional and increasingly disconnected, even in some ways estranged, from civilian society. Yet in comparison to previous peacetime professional forces, which were also isolated from civilian culture, today's are far larger, far more involved worldwide, far more capable, and often indispensable (even on a daily basis) to American foreign policy and world politics. Five decades of warfare and struggle against communism, moreover, have created something entirely new in American history—a separate military community, led by the regular forces but including also the National Guard and reserves, veterans organizations, and the communities, labor sectors, industries, and pressure groups active in military affairs. More diverse than the "military-industrial complex" of President Eisenhower's farewell address forty years ago, this "military" has become a recognizable interest group. Also, it is larger, more bureaucratically active, more political, more partisan, more purposeful, and more influential than anything similar in American history.[53]

One might argue that this is all temporary, the unique residue of sixty years of world and cold war, and that it will dissipate and balance will return now that the Clinton administration is history. Perhaps—but civil-military conflict is not very likely to diminish. In "Rumsfeld's Rules," Donald Rumsfeld states that his primary function is "to exercise civilian control over the Department for the Commander-in-Chief and the country." He understands that he possesses "the right to get into anything and exercise it [i.e., civilian control]." He recognizes as a rule, "When cutting staff at the Pentagon, don't eliminate the thin layer that assures civilian control."[54] Nonetheless, his effort to recast the military establishment for the post–Cold War era—as promised during the 2000 presidential campaign—provoked such immediate and powerful resistance (and not just by the armed forces) that he abandoned any plans to force reorganization or cut "legacy" weapons systems.[55] In the Afghanistan campaign, Rumsfeld and other civilian leaders have reportedly been frustrated by an apparent lack of imagination on the part of the military; in return, at least one four-star has accused Rumsfeld of "micromanagement."[56] There is also other evidence of conflict to come; traditional conceptions of military professionalism—particularly the ethical and professional norms of the officer corps—have been evolving away from concepts and behaviors that facilitate civil-military cooperation.

If the manifestations of diminished civilian control were simply a sine curve—that is, a low period in a recurring pattern—or the coincidence of a strong Joint Chiefs and a weak president during a critical transitional period in American history and national defense (the end of the Cold War), there would be little cause for concern. Civilian control, as we have seen, is situational and indeed to a degree cyclical. But the present decline extends back before the Clinton administration. There are indications that the current trend began before the Vietnam War and has since been aggravated by a weakening of the nation's social, political, and institutional structures that had, over the course of American history, assured civilian control.

For more than two centuries, civilian control has rested on four foundations that individually and in combination not only prevented any direct military threat to civilian government but kept military influence, even in wartime, largely contained within the boundaries of professional expertise and concerns. First has been the rule of law, and with it reverence for a constitution that provided explicitly for civilian control of the military. Any violation of the Constitution or its process has been sure to bring retribution from one or all three of the branches of government, with public support. Second, Americans once kept their regular forces small. The United States relied in peacetime on ocean boundaries to provide sufficient warning of attack and depended on a policy of mobilization to repel invasion or to wage war. Thus the regular military could never endanger civilian government—in peacetime because of its size, and in wartime because the ranks were filled with citizens unlikely to cooperate or acquiesce in anything illegal or unconstitutional. The very reliance on citizen soldiers—militia, volunteers, and conscripts pressed temporarily into service to meet an emergency—was a third safeguard of civilian control. Finally, the armed forces themselves internalized military subordination to civil authority. They accepted it willingly as an axiom of American government and the foundation of military professionalism. "You must remember that when we enter the army we do so with the full knowledge that our first duty is toward the government, entirely regardless of our own views under any given circumstances," Major General John J. Pershing instructed First Lieutenant George S. Patton, Jr., in 1916. "We are at liberty to express our personal views only when called upon to do so or else confidentially to our friends, but always confidentially and with the complete understanding that they are in no sense to govern our actions."[57] As Omar Bradley, the first chairman of the Joint Chiefs of Staff, put it, "Thirty-two years in the peacetime army had taught me to do my job, hold my tongue, and keep my name out of the papers."[58]

Much has changed. More than sixty years of hot and cold war, a large military establishment, world responsibilities, a searing failure in Vietnam, and changes in American society, among other factors, have weakened these four foundations upon which civilian control has rested in the United States.

The first, and most troubling, development is the skepticism, even cynicism, now expressed about government, lawyers, and justice, part of a broad and generation-long diminution of respect for people and institutions that has eroded

American civic culture and faith in law. Polling data show that Americans today have the most confidence in their least democratic institutions: the military, small business, the police, and the Supreme Court. Americans express the least confidence in the most democratic: Congress.[59] So dangerous is this trend that Harvard's Kennedy School of Government established a "Visions of Governance for the Twenty-first Century" project to explore the phenomenon, study its implications, and attempt to counteract some of its more deleterious effects.[60] Americans cannot continue to vilify government, the U.S. government in particular, and expect patriotism to prosper or even survive as a fundamental civic value.

Second, the media, traditionally the herald of liberty in this society, has become less substantial, more superficial, less knowledgeable, more focused on profit, less professional, and more trivial. About the only liberty the media seems to champion vocally is the freedom of the press. Issues of civilian control seem to escape the press; time after time, events or issues that in past years would have been framed or interpreted as touching upon civilian control now go unnoticed and unreported, at least in those terms.[61]

Third, the nation's core civic culture has deteriorated. Such basic social institutions as marriage and the family, and such indicators of society's health as crime rates and out-of-wedlock births, while stabilizing or improving in the 1990s, clearly have weakened over time. Our communities, neighborhoods, civic organizations, fraternal groups, and social gatherings have diminished in favor of individual entertainment; people are staying at home with cable television, the videocassette recorder, and the Internet, thereby avoiding crime, crowds, traffic, and the crumbling physical and social infrastructure of our society. American society has become more splintered and people more isolated into small groups, "clustered" geographically and demographically around similar values, culture, and lifestyles. With this deterioration of civic cohesion—gated communities being perhaps emblematic—has come a weakening of shared values: less truthfulness, less generosity, less sacrifice, less social consciousness, less faith, less common agreement on ethical behavior, and more advocacy, acrimony, individualism, relativism, materialism, cynicism, and self-gratification. The 11 September attacks and the war on terrorism are unlikely to reverse these trends as long as the national leadership exhorts the American people to go back to "normal."[62]

Civilian control is one common understanding that seems to have faded in American civic consciousness. The American people—whose study and understanding of civics and government generally have declined—have lost their traditional skepticism about the professional military that made civilian control a core political assumption, one that was widely understood and periodically voiced. Simply put, the public no longer thinks about civilian control—does not understand it, does not discuss it, and does not grasp how it can and should operate.[63] An occasional popular movie like *The Siege* and *Thirteen Days* raises the issue, but most recent films caricature the military or, like *GI Jane* and *Rules of Engagement*, lionize an honest, brave, faithful military and demonize lying, avaricious politicians.[64]

Fourth, in the last generation the United States has abandoned the first principle of civilian control, the bedrock practice extending back into premodern England—reliance on the citizen soldier for national defense.[65] National security policy no longer seriously envisions mobilizing industry and the population for large-scale war. Americans in uniform, whether they serve for one hitch or an entire career, are taught to (and do) view themselves as professionals. In the National Guard and reserves, whose members are thought to be the apotheosis of citizen soldiers, some hold civilian government jobs in their units or elsewhere in the government national security community, and others serve on active duty considerably more than the traditional one weekend a month and two weeks a year.[66]

Furthermore, while Guardsmen and reservists both voice and believe the traditional rhetoric about citizen-soldiering, the views of their up-and-coming officers mirror almost exactly those of their regular counterparts.[67] Reserve forces are spending more and more time on active duty, not simply for temporary duty for the present crisis of homeland defense. Increasingly, the National Guard and reserves are being used interchangeably with the regulars, even in overseas deployments on constabulary missions, something wholly unprecedented.[68] Even if they call themselves citizen soldiers, the fundamental distinction between citizens and soldiers has so blurred that in 1998, at two of the most respected U.S. institutions of professional military education, Marine majors who had spent their adult lives in uniform and National Guard adjutant generals who had done the same could both insist that they were "citizen soldiers."[69] Americans have lost the high regard they once possessed for temporary military service as an obligation of citizenship, along with their former understanding of its underlying contribution to civic cohesion and civilian control of the military.[70]

Today, fewer Americans serve or know people who do, and the numbers will decline as smaller percentages of the population serve in uniform.[71] Their sense of ownership of or interest in the military, and their understanding of the distinctiveness of military culture—its ethos and needs—have declined. In recent years the number of veterans serving in the U.S. Congress has fallen 50 percent, and the remaining veterans constitute a smaller percentage of the members of Congress than veterans do of the population as a whole, reversing (in 1995) a pattern that had endured since the turn of the century.[72] The effect is dramatic; less than ten years ago, 62 percent of the Senate and 41 percent of the House were veterans. Today in the 107th Congress, the figure for the Senate is 38 percent, and for the House, 29 percent.[73]

Finally, at the same time that civilian control has weakened in the awareness of the public, so too has the principle declined in the consciousness and professional understanding of the American armed forces. Historically, one of the chief bulwarks of civilian control has been the American military establishment itself. Its small size in peacetime, the professionalism of the officers, their political neutrality, their willing subordination, and their acceptance of a set of unwritten but largely understood rules of behavior in the civil-military relationship—all had made civilian control succeed, messy as it sometimes was and situational as it must always be. In the last half-century, however, while everyone in the armed forces has continued to support the concept, the ethos and *mentalité* of the officer corps have changed in ways that damage civil-military cooperation and undermine civilian control.

Reversing a century and a half of practice, the American officer corps has become partisan in political affiliation, and overwhelmingly Republican. Beginning with President Richard Nixon's politics of polarization—the "southern strategy" and reaching out to the "hard-hats"—Republicans embraced traditional patriotism and strong national defense as central parts of their national agenda. During the late 1970s—years of lean defense budgets and the "hollow force"—and in the 1980s, when Ronald Reagan made rebuilding the armed forces and taking the offensive in the Cold War centerpieces of his presidency, Republicans reached out to the military as a core constituency. They succeeded in part because, in the wake of Vietnam, the Democratic Party virtually abandoned the military, offering antimilitary rhetoric and espousing reduced defense spending. During the same period, voting in elections began to become a habit in the officer corps. In the 1950s, the Federal Voting Assistance Program came into existence in order to help enlisted men, most of whom were draftees or draft-induced volunteers, to vote. In every unit an officer was designated to connect the program to the men, and undoubtedly the task began to break down slowly what had been something of a taboo against officers exercising their franchise. How (the logic must have been) could officers encourage their soldiers to vote if they themselves abstained?[74]

Today the vast majority of officers not only vote but identify with a political philosophy and party. Comparison of a sample by the Triangle Institute of Security Studies of active-duty officers (see endnote 25) with earlier data shows a shift from over 54 percent independent, "no preference," or "other" in a 1976 survey to 28 percent in 1998–99, and from 33 percent to 64 percent Republican today.[75] In the presidential election of 2000, Republicans targeted military voters by organizing endorsements from retired flag officers, advertising in military publications, using Gulf War heroes Colin Powell and H. Norman Schwarzkopf on the campaign trail, urging service members to register and vote, and focusing special effort on absentee military voters—a group that proved critical, perhaps the margin of victory, in Florida, where thousands of armed forces personnel maintain their legal residency.[76]

Before the present generation, American military officers (since before the Civil War) had abstained as a group from party politics, studiously avoiding any partisanship of word or deed, activity, or affiliation. By George C. Marshall's time, the practice was not even to vote.[77] A handful of the most senior officers pursued political ambitions, usually trying to parlay wartime success into the presidency. A very few even ran for office while on active duty. But these were exceptions. The belief was that the military, as the neutral servant of the state, stood above the dirty business of politics. Professional norms dictated faith and loyalty not just in deed but in spirit to whoever held the reins of power under the constitutional system. For Marshall's generation, partisan affiliation and voting conflicted with military professionalism.[78]

Marshall and his fellow officers must have sensed that the habit of voting leads to partisan thinking, inclining officers to become invested in particular policy choices or decisions that relate directly to their professional responsibilities.[79] Officers at every level have to bring difficult and sometimes unpopular duties to their troops and motivate the latter to carry them out. Likewise, senior officers must represent the needs and perspectives of the troops to political leaders even when they are unsolicited or unwanted. How effective can that advice be if the civilians know the officers are opposed to a policy in question? What are the effects on morale when the troops know their officers dislike, disrespect, or disagree with the politicians, or think a mission is unwise, ill conceived, or unnecessary?

The consequences of partisanship can also be more subtle and indirect but equally far-reaching, even to the point of contempt for civilian policy and politicians or of unprofessional, disruptive behavior, as in 1993. The belief is current today among officers that the core of the Democratic Party is "hostile to military culture" and engaged in a "culture war" against the armed forces, mostly because of pressure for further gender integration and open homosexual service.[80] During the 2000 election campaign, when Al Gore stumbled briefly by supporting a "litmus test" on gays in the military for selecting members of the Joint Chiefs, he confirmed for many in uniform the idea that Democrats do

George C. Marshall
(G.C. Marshall Foundation)

not understand the military profession or care about its effectiveness. His campaign's effort to minimize the effect of absentee votes in Florida and elsewhere through technical challenges outraged the armed forces, raising worries that a Gore victory might spark an exodus from the ranks or that a Gore administration would have relations with the military even more troubled than Clinton's.[81]

Partisan politicization loosens the connection of the military to the American people. If the public begins to perceive the military as an interest group driven by its own needs and agenda, support—and trust—will diminish. Already there are hints. When a random survey asked a thousand Americans in the fall of 1998 how often military leaders would try to avoid carrying out orders they opposed, over two-thirds answered at least "some of the time."[82]

Partisanship also poisons the relationship between the president and the uniformed leadership. When a group of retired flag officers, including former regional commanders and members of the Joint Chiefs, endorsed presidential candidates in 1992 and again in 2000, they broadcast their politicization to the public and further legitimated partisanship in the ranks—for everyone knows that four-stars never really retire. Like princes of the church, they represent the culture and the profession just as authoritatively as their counterparts on active duty. If senior retired officers make a practice of endorsing presidential contenders, will the politicians trust the generals and admirals on active duty, in particular those who serve at the top, to have the loyalty and discretion not to retire and use their inside knowledge to try to overturn policies or elect opponents? Will not presidents begin to vet candidates for the top jobs for their pliability or (equally deleteriously) their party or political views, rather than for excellence, achievement, character, and candor? Over time, the result will be weak military advice, declining military effectiveness, and accelerating politicization.

The investment of officers in one policy or another will lead civilians to question whether military recommendations are the best professional advice of the nation's military experts. Perhaps one reason Bill Clinton and his people dealt with the military at arm's length was that he and they knew that officers were the most solidly Republican group in the government.[83] One need only read Richard Holbrooke's memoir about negotiating the Dayton accords in 1995 to plumb the depth of suspicion between military and civilian at the highest levels. Convinced that the military opposed the limited bombing campaign against the Bosnian Serbs, Holbrooke and Secretary of State Warren Christopher believed that the vice chairman of the Joint Chiefs was lying to them when he asserted that the Air Force was running out of targets.[84]

Certainly officers have the right to vote and to participate privately in the nation's political life. No one questions the legal entitlement of retired officers to run for office or endorse candidates. But these officers must recognize the corrosive effects on military professionalism and the threat to the military establishment's relationship with Congress, the executive branch, and the American people that such partisan behavior has. Possessing a right and exercising it are two very different things.

A second example of changing military professionalism has been the widespread attitude among officers that civilian society has become corrupt, even degenerate, while the military has remained a repository for virtue, perhaps its one remaining bastion, in an increasingly unraveling social fabric, of the traditional values that make the country strong. Historically, officers have often decried the selfishness, commercialism, and disorder that seems to characterize much of American society.[85] But that opinion today has taken on a harder, more critical, more moralistic edge; it is less leavened by that sense of acceptance that enabled officers in the past to tolerate the clash between their values and those of a democratic, individualistic civilian culture and to reconcile the conflict with their own continued service.

Nearly 90 percent of the elite military officers (regular and reserves) surveyed in 1998–99 by the Triangle Institute for Security Studies agreed that "the decline of traditional values is contributing to the breakdown of our society." Some 70 percent thought that "through leading by example, the military could help American society become more moral," and 75 percent believed that "civilian society would be better off if it adopted more of the military's values and customs."[86] Is it healthy for civilian control when the members of the American armed forces believe that they are morally, organizationally, institutionally, and personally superior to the rest of society—and are contemptuous of that society? Do we wish civic society in a democratic country to adopt military norms, values, outlooks, and behaviors? In my judgment that is an utter misreading of the role and function of our armed forces. Their purpose is to defend society, not to define it. The latter is militarism, in the classic definition—the same thinking that in part inclined the French and German armies to intervene in the politics of their nations in the twentieth century.

A third, and most disturbing, change in military sentiment is the belief that officers should confront and resist civilians whose policies or decisions they believe threaten to weaken national defense or lead the country into disaster. Many hold that officers should speak out publicly, or work behind the scenes, to stop or modify a policy, or resign in protest. Some senior leaders have been willing to speak publicly on issues of national security, foreign relations, and military policy before it is formulated, and afterward as spokespersons for what are often highly controversial and partisan initiatives or programs. In 1998 and 1999, the respected retired Army colonel and political scientist Sam Sarkesian, and the much-decorated Marine veteran, novelist, and former secretary of the Navy James Webb, called publicly for military leaders to participate in national security policy debates, not merely as advisers to the civilian leadership but as public advocates, an idea that seems to resonate with many in the armed forces today.[87] "Military subservience to political control applies to existing policy, not to policy debates," admonished Webb—as if officers can subscribe to policy and debate it honestly at the same time.[88] Such behavior politicizes military issues and professional officers directly, for rare is the military issue that remains insulated from politics and broader national life.

This willingness—indeed, in some cases eagerness—to strive to shape public opinion and thereby affect decisions and policy outcomes is a dangerous development for the U.S. military and is extraordinarily corrosive of civilian control. Is it proper for military officers to leak information to the press "to discredit specific policies—procurement decisions, prioritization plans, operations that the leaker opposes," as Admiral Crowe in his memoirs admits happens "sometimes," even "copiously"?[89] Is it proper for the four services, the regional commanders, or the Joint Chiefs every year to advocate to the public directly their needs for ships, airplanes, divisions, troops, and other resources, or their views on what percentage of the nation's economy should go to defense as opposed to other priorities?[90] This advocacy reached such a cacophony in the fall of 2000 that the secretary of defense warned the military leadership not "to beat the drum with a tin cup" for their budgets during the presidential campaign and the transition to a new administration.[91]

Do we wish the military leadership to argue the merits of intervention in the Balkans or elsewhere, of whether to sign treaties on land-mine use or war crimes, in order to mobilize public opinion one way or the other, before the president decides? Imagine that we are back in 1941. Should the Army and the Navy pronounce publicly on the merits or demerits of Lend-Lease, or convoy escort, or the occupation of Iceland, or the Europe-first strategy? Or imagine it is 1861—should the nation's military leaders publicly discuss whether to reinforce Fort Sumter? Would it be advisable for senior officers to proclaim openly their varied opinions of whether the South's secession ought to (or can) be opposed by plunging the country into civil war? Should senior military officers question the president's strategy in the midst of a military operation, as was done in 1999 through media leaks in the first week of the bombing campaign over Kosovo?[92] In such instances, what happens to the president's, and Congress's, authority and credibility with the public, and to their ability to lead the nation? How does such advocacy affect the trust and confidence between the president, his cabinet officers, and the most senior generals and admirals, trust and confidence that is so necessary for effective national defense?[93]

The way in which military officers have interpreted a study of the role of the Joint Chiefs of Staff in the decision on intervention and in the formulation of strategy for Southeast Asia in 1963–65 exemplifies the erosion of professional norms and values. H. R. McMaster's *Dereliction of Duty: Lyndon Johnson, Robert McNamara, the Joint Chiefs of Staff and the Lies That Led to Vietnam* is by all accounts the history book most widely read and discussed in the military in the last several years.[94] Officers believe that McMaster validates long-standing military convictions about Vietnam—that the Joint Chiefs, lacking a proper understanding of their role and not having the courage to oppose the Johnson administration's strategy of gradualism that they knew would fail, should have voiced their opposition, publicly if necessary, and resigned rather than carry out that strategy. Had they done so, goes this credo, they would have saved the country a tragic, costly, humiliating, and above all, unnecessary, defeat.[95]

McMaster's book neither says nor implies that the chiefs should have obstructed U.S. policy in Vietnam in any other way than by presenting their views frankly and forcefully to their civilian superiors, and speaking honestly to the Congress when asked for their views. It neither states nor suggests that the chiefs should have opposed President Lyndon Johnson's orders and policies by leaks, public statements, or by resignations, unless an officer personally and professionally could not stand, morally and ethically, to carry out the chosen policy. There is in fact no tradition of resignation in the American military. In 1783, at Newburgh, New York, as the war for independence was ending, the American officer corps rejected individual or mass resignation—which can be indistinguishable from mutiny. George Washington persuaded them not to march on Congress or refuse orders in response to congressional unwillingness to pay them or guarantee their hard-earned pensions. The precedent has survived for more than two centuries. No American army ever again considered open insubordination.

Proper professional behavior cannot include simply walking away from a policy, an operation, or a war an officer believes is wrong or will fail. That is what the Left advocated during the Vietnam War, and the American military rightly rejected it. Imagine the consequences if the Union army had decided in late 1862 that it had signed on to save the Union but not to free the slaves and had resigned en masse because of disagreement (which was extensive) with the Emancipation Proclamation. More recently, Air Force chief of

Lyndon Baines Johnson
(LBJ Library and Museum)

staff Ronald Fogleman did not resign in protest in 1997, as many officers wish to believe; he requested early retirement and left in such a manner—quietly, without a full explanation—precisely so as *not* to confront his civilian superior over a decision with which he deeply disagreed.[96] All McMaster says (and believes), and all that is proper in the American system, is that military officers should advise honestly and forthrightly, or advocate in a confidential capacity, a course of action. Whether their advice is heeded or not, if the policy or decision is legal, they are to carry it out.

Resignation in protest directly assails civilian control. Issuing a public explanation for resignation, however diplomatically couched, amounts to marshaling all of an officer's military knowledge, expertise, and experience—as well as the profession's standing with the public and reputation for disinterested patriotism—to undercut some undertaking or concept that the officer opposes. The fact that officers today either ignore or are oblivious to this basic aspect of their professional ethics and would countenance, even admire, such truculent behavior illustrates both a fundamental misunderstanding of civilian control and its weakening as a primary professional value.[97]

Our military leaders have already traveled far in the direction of self-interested bureaucratic behavior in the last half-century, to become advocates for policy outcomes as opposed to advisers—presenting not only the military perspective on a problem, or the needs of the military establishment and national defense, or the interests of their services or branches, but their own views of foreign and military policy—even, as we have seen, pressing these efforts outside the normal advisory channels. Some of this is unthinking, some the product of civilian abrogation of responsibility, and some is the unintended consequence of the Goldwater-Nichols Act, which so strengthened the chairman and the regional commanders. But let us be clear: some is quite conscious. In his memoirs, Colin Powell, the most celebrated soldier of the era, wrote that he learned as a White House Fellow, from his most important mentor, that in the government "you never know what you can get away with until you try."[98] Is that a proper standard of professional behavior for a uniformed officer? He also declared that his generation of officers "vowed that when our turn came to call the shots, we would not quietly acquiesce in halfhearted warfare for half-baked reasons that the American people could not understand or support."[99] Is that a proper view of military subordination to civilian authority?

Unfortunately, General Powell's views mirror attitudes that have become widespread over the last generation. The survey of officer and civilian attitudes and opinions undertaken by the Triangle Institute in 1998–99 discovered that many officers believe that they have the duty to force their own views on civilian decision makers when the United States is contemplating committing American forces abroad. When "asked whether . . . military leaders should be neutral, advise, advocate, or insist on having their way in . . . the decision process" to use military force, 50 percent or more of the up-and-coming active-duty officers answered "insist," on the following issues: "setting rules of engagement, ensuring that clear political and military goals exist . . . , developing an 'exit strategy,'" and "deciding what kinds of military units . . . will be used to accomplish all tasks."[100] In the context of the questionnaire, "insist" definitely implied that officers should try to compel acceptance of the military's recommendations.

In 2000, a three-star general casually referred to a uniformed culture in the Pentagon that labels the Office of the Secretary of Defense as "the enemy"—because it exercises civilian control.[101] In 1999, staff officers of the National Security Council deliberately attempted to promulgate a new version of the national security strategy quickly enough to prevent the president from enunciating his own principles first.[102] In 1997 the chairman of the Joint Chiefs urged the chiefs to block Congress's effort to reform the military establishment through the Quadrennial Defense Review.[103] In the early 1990s, senior officers presented alternatives for the use of American forces abroad specifically designed to discourage the civilian leadership from intervening in the first place.[104] Twice in the past five years members of the Joint Chiefs have threatened to resign as a means of blocking a policy or decision.[105]

Thus, in the last generation, the American military has slipped from conceiving of its primary role as advice to civilians followed by execution of their orders, to trying—as something proper, even essential in some situations—to impose its viewpoint on policies or decisions. In other words, American officers have, over the course of the Cold War and in reaction to certain aspects of it, forgotten or abandoned their historical stewardship of civilian control, their awareness of the requirement to maintain it, and their understanding of the proper boundaries and behaviors that made it work properly and effectively. That so many voices applaud this behavior or sanction it by their silence suggests that a new definition of military professionalism may be forming, at least in civil-military relations. If so, the consequences are not likely to benefit national security; they could alter the character of American government itself.

Even military readers who accept my presentation of facts may find my concerns overblown. Certainly, there is no crisis. The American military conceives of itself as loyal and patriotic; it universally expresses support for civilian control as a fundamental principle of government and of military professionalism. Yet at the same time, the evidence is overwhelming that civil-military relationships have deteriorated in the U.S. government. The underlying structures of civilian society and the military profession that traditionally supported the system of civilian control have weakened. Over the course of the last generation, much influence and actual power has migrated to the military, which has either been allowed to define, or has itself claimed, an expanded role in foreign policy and national security decision making.[106] The reasons are complex—partly circumstance, partly civilian inattention or politically motivated timidity. But a further reason is that military leaders have either forgotten or chosen to ignore the basic behaviors by which civil-military relations support military effectiveness and civilian control at the same time. Whatever the causes, the consequences are dangerous. Increased military influence, combined with the American people's ignorance of or indifference to civilian control and the misreading of the bounds of professional behavior on the part of senior military officers, could in the future produce a civil-military clash that damages American government or compromises the nation's defense.

> *"The dirty little secret of American civil-military relations . . . is that the commander in chief does not command the military establishment; he cajoles it, negotiates with it, and, as necessary, appeases it."*

That civilians in the executive and legislative branches of government over the last generation bear ultimate responsibility for these developments is beyond doubt. Some on both sides seem to sense it. Secretaries of defense came into office in 1989, 1993, and 2001 concerned about military subordination and determined to exert their authority. Civilian officials have the obligation to make the system work, not to abdicate for any reason. But to rely on the politicians to restore the proper balance is to ignore the conditions and processes that can frustrate civilian control. The historical record is not encouraging. Over two centuries, the officials elected and appointed to rule the military have varied enormously in knowledge, experience, understanding, and motivation. Their propensity to exercise civilian control and to provide sound, forceful leadership has been variable, largely situational, and unpredictable.[107]

Nor can the changes in American society and political understanding that have weakened civilian control be easily reversed. National defense will capture at best superficial public attention even during a war on terrorism, unless military operations are ongoing or the government asks for special sacrifice. In wartime, Americans want to rely more on military advice and authority, not less. Over time, a smaller and smaller percentage of Americans are likely to perform military service; without a conscious effort by the media to avoid caricaturing military culture, and by colleges and universities to expand programs in military history and security studies, future generations of civilian leaders will lack not only the experience of military affairs but the comprehension of the subject needed to make civilian control work effectively.

A better way to alter the equation is for officers to recall the attitudes and rejuvenate the behaviors that civilian control requires. Certainly every officer supports the concept; every officer swears at commissioning "to support and defend the Constitution of the United States" and to "bear true faith and allegiance" to the same.[108] Because civilian control pervades the Constitution, the oath is a personal promise to preserve, protect, defend, and support civilian control, in actual practice as well as in words. The requirement for such an oath was written into the Constitution for precisely that purpose.[109] Officers do not swear to strive to maximize their services' budgets, or to try to achieve certain policy outcomes, or to attempt to reshape civilian life toward a military vision of the good society.

Individual officers at every level would do well to examine their personal views of civilians, particularly of their clients: the American people, elected officials, and those appointed to exercise responsibility in national security affairs. A certain amount of caution, skepticism, and perhaps even mistrust is healthy. But contempt for clients destroys the professional relationship. Lawyers cannot provide sound counsel, doctors effective treatment, ministers worthwhile support, teachers significant education—when they do not understand and respect their clients. Military officers who feel contempt for their elected or appointed supervisors, or the voters who placed them in office, are unlikely to advise them wisely or carry out their policies effectively.

Officers should investigate their own professional views of civilian control. On what do you base your thinking? Much of the problem I have discussed may stem from the Cold War, or from one particular campaign of it, Vietnam, which continues to cast a long, if sometimes unnoticed, shadow. Are you positive that your thinking about civil-military relations does not rest on the mistaken beliefs—and they *are* mistaken—that the war was lost because of too much civilian control, or that we succeeded so magnificently in the Persian Gulf in 1991 because the civilians "[got] out of the way and let the military fight and win the war"?[110] Neither of those interpretations fit the facts of what happened in either war.[111]

Ponder whether you are prepared to accept, as a principle of civilian control, that it includes the right of civilians to be wrong, to make mistakes—indeed, to insist on making mistakes.[112] This may be very hard to accept, given that people's lives, or the security of the nation, hang in the balance. But remember that the military can be wrong, dead wrong, about military affairs—for after all, you are not politicians, and as Carl von Clausewitz wrote long ago, war is an extension of politics.[113] Were you prepared to work for and with, and to accept, a Gore administration had the Democratic candidate won the 2000 election? If there is doubt on your part, ponder the implications for civil-military relations and civilian control. It is likely that within the next dozen years, there will be another

Democratic administration. If the trend toward increasing friction and hostility in civil-military relations during the last three—those of Johnson, Carter, and Clinton—continues into the future, the national security of the United States will not be well served.

Last of all, consider that if civilian control is to function effectively, the uniformed military will have not only to forswear or abstain from certain behavior but actively encourage civilians to exercise their authority and perform their legal and constitutional duty to make policy and decisions. You cannot and will not solve those problems yourselves, nor is it your responsibility alone. Civilian behavior and historical circumstances are just as much the causes of the present problems in civil-military relations as any diminution of military professionalism. But you can help educate and develop civilian leaders in their roles and on the processes of policy making, just as your predecessors did, by working with them and helping them—without taking advantage of them, even when the opportunity arises. Proper professional behavior calls for a certain amount of abstinence. What is being asked of you is no more or less than is asked of other professionals who must subordinate their self-interest when serving their clients and customers: lawyers to act against their self-interest and advise clients not to press frivolous claims; doctors not to prescribe treatments that are unnecessary; accountants to audit their clients' financial statements fully and honestly; clergymen to refrain from exploiting the trust of parishioners or congregants.[114] It will be up to you to shape the relationship with your particular client, just as others do. At its heart, the relationship involves civilian control in fact as well as form.

Civilian control ultimately must be considered in broad context. In the long history of human civilization, there have been military establishments that have focused on external defense—on protecting their societies—and those that have preyed upon their own populations.[115] The American military has never preyed on this society. Yet democracy, as a widespread form of governance, is rather a recent phenomenon, and our country has been fortunate to be perhaps the leading example for the rest of the world. For us, civilian control has been more a matter of making certain the civilians control military affairs than of keeping the military out of civilian politics. But if the United States is to teach civilian control—professional military behavior—to countries overseas, its officers must look hard at their own system and their own behavior at the same time.[116] Our government must champion civilian control in all circumstances, without hesitation. In April 2002 the United States acted with stupefying and self-defeating hypocrisy when the White House initially expressed pleasure at the apparent overthrow of President Hugo Chavez in Venezuela by that country's military, condoning an attempted coup while other nations in the hemisphere shunned the violation of democratic and constitutional process.[117] "No one pretends that democracy is perfect or all-wise," Winston Churchill shrewdly observed in 1947. "Indeed, it has been said that democracy is the worst form of Government except all those other forms that have been tried."[118] Churchill certainly knew the tensions involved in civil-military relations as well as any democratic head of government in modern history. Both sides—civilian and military—need to be conscious of these problems and to work to ameliorate them.

NOTES

1. Defenders of the chiefs' behavior in the 1992–93 firestorm over gays in the military often assert that the Clinton administration's intention to lift the ban on homosexual service was blocked not by the military but by Congress. However, military leaders very clearly encouraged their retired predecessors to lobby the Congress against Clinton's intentions. "The word went out to the senior retirees," recalls a knowledgeable, well-connected retired Army brigadier general; "'We've lost unless you can generate enough pressure on Congress to block this.'" Theodore Metaxis to the author, 24 October 1999. See also Theo. C. Metaxis, "Discipline, Morale Require Ban on Homosexuals," *Fayetteville (North Carolina) Observer-Times*, 28 January 1993, p. 15A, especially the closing two paragraphs, in which Metaxis calls on the public to "let the president and Congress know how you feel" and on the military to "put on your 'civilian hat,' the one you wear when you vote. Write your friends and relatives and let them know how you feel, and ask them to write to Washington. Then sit down and write to the president and Congress—let them know how you personally feel. For the officers and NCOs, tell them how your responsibility to command will be eroded. For the soldiers living in barracks, since the Clinton administration just doesn't 'get it,' call or write to them, explaining what the effect would be on you. If you don't take action, the torrent of PR publicity from the homosexual lobby may carry the day." See also Eric Schmitt, "The Top Soldier Is Torn between 2 Loyalties," *New York Times*, 6 February 1993, p. 1; "Aspin Seeks a Deal on Gays That the Brass Will Bless,"

" *Congressional Quarterly*, 26 June 1993, p. 1670; Eric Schmitt and Thomas L. Friedman, "Clinton and Powell Forge Bond for Mutual Survival," *New York Times*, 4 June 1993, p. 1; Richard Lacayo, "The Rebellious Soldier," *Time*, 15 February 1993, p. 32; Janet E. Halley, *Don't: A Reader's Guide to the Military's Anti-Gay Policy* (Durham, N.C.: Duke Univ. Press, 1999), pp. 20–5. The extent of the president's defeat is revealed in George Stephanopoulos, *All Too Human: A Political Education* (Boston: Little, Brown, 1999), pp. 155–63; Elizabeth Drew, *On the Edge: The Clinton Presidency* (New York: Simon and Schuster, 1994), pp. 42–8, 248–51.

2. Quoted in John Lancaster, "Air Force General Demands Tight Formation for Commander in Chief," *Washington Post*, 22 April 1993, p. 1, and "Accused of Ridiculing Clinton, General Faces Air Force Probe," *Washington Post*, 8 June 1993, p. 21. See also "The President and the General," 11 June 1993, p. 20, and "Transcript of President Clinton's News Conference," 16 June 1993, p. 14, both *Washington Post*; "A Military Breach?" *Seattle Post-Intelligencer*, 11 June 1993, p. 10; David H. Hackworth, "Rancor in the Ranks: The Troops vs. the President," *Newsweek*, 28 June 1993, p. 24; and Associated Press, "General's Lampoon of Clinton Not His First," *Washington Times*, 8 July 1993, p. 5.

3. The events described below were covered extensively in the daily press, journals of opinion, and other local and national media, 1993–2001.

4. The vitriol on gender and sexual orientation is revealed by Stephanie Gutman, *The Kinder,*

Gentler Military: Can America's Gender-Neutral Fighting Force Still Win Wars? (New York: Scribner's, 2000).

5. The arguments over readiness became so ugly by 1998 that the Joint Chiefs and U.S. senators engaged in public accusations of dishonest testimony and lack of support. See Eric Schmitt, "Joint Chiefs Accuse Congress of Weakening U.S. Defense," *New York Times*, 30 September 1998, p. 1. The military opposition to Clinton's interventions was almost immediate; see Richard A. Serrano and Art Pine, "Many in Military Angry over Clinton's Policies," *Los Angeles Times* (Washington ed.), 19 October 1993, p. 1. The arguments over readiness continued. See Elaine M. Grossman, "Congressional Aide Finds Spending on 'Core Readiness' in Decline," *Inside the Pentagon*, 28 June 2001, p. 1.

6. Rowan Scarborough, "Marine Officer Probed for Blasting Clinton," *Washington Times*, 11 November 1998, p. 1, and "Major Gets Punished for Criticizing President," *Washington Times*, 7 December 1998, p. 1; C. J. Chivers, "Troops Obey Clinton despite Disdain," *USA Today*, 18 November 1998, p. 27A; Pat Towell, "Keeping a Civil Tongue," *CQ Weekly*, 2 January 1999, p. 26. Article 88, "Contempt toward officials," reads: "Any commissioned officer who uses contemptuous words against the President, the Vice President, Congress, the Secretary of Defense, the Secretary of a military department, the Secretary of Transportation, or the Governor or the legislature of any State, Territory, Commonwealth, or possession in which he is on active duty or present shall be punished as a court-martial may direct." U.S. Defense Dept., *Manual for Courts-Martial United States (1995 Edition)* (Washington, D.C.: Joint Service Committee on Military Justice, 1995), pp. A2–A23. The history of this provision and its enforcement is covered in John G. Kester, "Soldiers Who Insult the President: An Uneasy Look at Article 88 of the Uniform Code of Military Justice," *Harvard Law Review*, vol. 81, 1967–68, pp. 1697–769; Daniel Blumenthal, "A Brief Overview of Article 88 of the Uniform Code of Military Justice," Strategy and Policy Seminar, Johns Hopkins School of Advanced International Studies, Washington, D.C., 4 December 1998.

7. "Wicked Wit," *New York Post*, 11 October 1999, p. 6.

8. Thomas E. Ricks, "Military Personnel Warned on Politics," *Washington Post*, 30 November 2000, p. 35. An Army officer, receiving the reminder by mass distribution in his command, recalled that "this was perhaps the fourth or fifth time in the past 8 years [i.e., the Clinton administration] that I have received some official reminder of Article 88." E-mail to the author, 27 November 2000. See also Robert G. Bracknell [Capt., USMC], "The Marine Officer's Moral and Legal Imperative of Political Abstinence," *Marine Corps Gazette*, September 2000, pp. 102–7.

9. Another major embarrassment singed the new administration when a female civilian staffer insulted Army lieutenant general Barry McCaffrey, a much-decorated and thrice-wounded veteran of Vietnam and commander of the 24th Infantry Division in the Gulf War. McCaffrey was then serving as assistant to the chairman of the Joint Chiefs of Staff. In response to a casual "good morning" in the White House, the staffer replied something to the effect of "We [or I] don't talk to people in uniform." Within hours the incident ricocheted all over Washington and into the press, to the mortification of the administration. The impact of this insult was felt most acutely inside the Washington Beltway, and especially in the officer corps. Kenneth T. Walsh, Bruce B. Auster, and Tim Zimmermann, "Clinton's Warrior Woes," *U.S. News and World Report*, 15 March 1993, pp. 22ff.; Carl M. Cannon, "Military Feeling Resentful toward the White House," *Buffalo (New York) News*, 23 March 1993, p. 5. McCaffrey was one of the officers featured in James Kitfield, *Prodigal Soldiers* (New York: Simon and Schuster, 1995); see also Jay Nordlinger, "Clinton's Good Soldier," *National Review*, 3 May 1999, pp. 20–3.

10. Conversation with a senior official, Office of the Secretary of Defense, April 1993.

11. President Clinton undertook from the beginning to woo the military, in an attempt to overcome the hostility. Walsh et al., "Clinton's Warrior Woes," p. 22; Carl M. Cannon, "Clinton Reaches for Military Trust," *Baltimore Sun*, 30 May 1992, p. 22. But five years later, the relationship was hardly better than "a wary truce." "I can't

think of any one thing the president has put more personal attention and caring into than his relationship with the military at all levels," White House press secretary Michael McCurry was quoted as saying. "He did it because he understood that he began with a significant deficit. He has tried to make a personal and human connection with his commanders and all the way down the chain." Brian McGrory, "U.S. Military, Clinton Achieve a Wary Truce," *Boston Globe*, 22 February 1998, p. 1. Indeed, two four-star officers having professional relationships with Clinton praised his discharge of his duties as commander in chief. See Richard H. Kohn, ed., "The Early Retirement of General Ronald R. Fogleman, Chief of Staff, United States Air Force," *Aerospace Power Journal*, Spring 2001, p. 16; Wesley K. Clark [Gen., USA], *Waging Modern War: Bosnia, Kosovo, and the Future of Combat* (New York: PublicAffairs, 2001), p. 290. However, the "personal and human connection" apparently never altered the Clinton-hating in the officer corps generally, which lasted for both his terms. See David Halberstam, *War in a Time of Peace: Bush, Clinton, and the Generals* (New York: Scribner's, 2001), pp. 415–9; Joseph Curl, "Military Finds Refreshing Change with New Commander in Chief," *Washington Times*, 13 February 2001, p. 1. For the economic trade emphasis of the administration's foreign policy, see Halberstam, *War in a Time of Peace*, p. 242; David E. Sanger, "Economic Engine for Foreign Policy," *New York Times*, 28 December 2000, p. A1. Scholarly analyses of the Clinton foreign policy are William C. Berman, *From the Center to the Edge: The Politics and Policies of the Clinton Presidency* (Lanham, Md.: Rowman and Littlefield, 2001), pp. 35–8; Andrew J. Bacevich, *American Empire: The Realities and Consequences of U.S. Diplomacy* (Cambridge, Mass.: Harvard Univ. Press, in press [due fall 2002]).

12. Jane Perlez, "For 8 Years, a Strained Relationship with the Military," *New York Times*, 28 December 2000, p. A13.

13. "Clinton and the Generals," *Vanity Fair*, September 2001, p. 230.

14. In 1996, former congressman and secretary of defense (and now vice president) Dick Cheney observed: "If you look at the '92 election, the '94 congressional election, and I think even the 1996 presidential election, there has been almost no discussion—this will be the third election cycle without it—of the U.S. role in the world from a security standpoint, or strategic requirements, what our military ought to be doing, or how big the defense budget ought to be." Quoted in Stephen M. Duncan, *Citizen Warriors: America's National Guard and Reserve Forces and the Politics of National Security* (Novato, Calif.: Presidio, 1997), p. 225.

15. The most insightful brief analysis of the overall character of the military establishment is Eliot A. Cohen, "Defending America in the Twenty-first Century," *Foreign Affairs*, November/ December 2000, pp. 40–56. For another persuasive argument for continuity with the Cold War establishment, see William Greider, *Fortress America: The American Military and the Consequences of Peace* (New York: PublicAffairs, 1998).

16. Michael R. Gordon, "Cuts Force Review of War Strategies," *New York Times*, 30 May 1993, p. 16. Barton Gellman, "Rumblings of Discord Heard in Pentagon; Aspin's Civilian Leadership, Management Style and Agenda Irk Some Officers," *Washington Post*, 20 June 1993, p. 1; John Lancaster, "Aspin Opts for Winning 2 Wars—Not 1½—at Once; Practical Effect of Notion Is Uncertain amid Huge Military Budget Cuts," *Washington Post*, 25 June 1993, p. A6. For a broad analysis of the Bottom-Up Review, see Donald Kagan and Frederick W. Kagan, *While America Sleeps: Self-Delusion, Military Weakness, and the Threat to Peace Today* (New York: St. Martin's, 2000), chap. 14.

17. The disjunction between resources and requirements, which became the subject of much debate and recrimination in the late 1990s, was clear by 1995. See Daniel Gouré and Jeffrey M. Ranney, *Averting the Defense Train Wreck in the New Millennium* (Washington, D.C.: Center for Strategic and International Studies, 1999), p. 1; Don M. Snider, "The Coming Defense Train Wreck," *Washington Quarterly*, Winter 1996, 89–101, with commentary on "what to do about it," pp. 103–24. Wesley Clark recalls that when he was a lieutenant general and head of plans (J-5) on the Joint Staff, beginning in 1994, "We had constructed a closed cycle

bureaucratic instrument that would focus the U.S. Armed Forces' thinking on only two primary conflicts and then drive marginal investments of scarce resources to enhance these capabilities at the expense of other possible employments." This "wasn't intended to be a strategy for employing the forces—it was meant to defend the size of the military." Clark, *Waging Modern War*, pp. 47, 36.

18. A brief analysis of these dilemmas is John F. Lehman and Harvey Sicherman, "Demilitarizing the Military," Foreign Policy Research Institute *Wire*, July 1997. More extended analyses are Gouré and Ranney, *Averting the Defense Train Wreck*, chaps. 1–2; and Greider, *Fortress America*, esp. pp. 28–9, 36–9, 42–5.

19. For recent indications of how electronics and miniaturization, leading to greater accuracy of weapons, faster acquisition of targets, and more comprehensive networking of computer systems, and the like, might be affecting warfare and the armed services, see James Kitfield, "The Permanent Frontier," *National Journal*, 17 March 2001, p. 780; Joseph Fitchett, "Spying from Space: U.S. to Sharpen the Focus," *International Herald Tribune*, 10 April 2001, p. 1; Glenn W. Goodman, Jr., "Futuristic Army Vision: The Service's Future Combat System Is a True Leap-Ahead Program," *Armed Forces Journal International*, May 2001, p. 26; James Ware, "Virtual Defense," *Foreign Affairs*, May/June 2001, pp. 98–112; Nicholas Lemann, "Dreaming about War," *The New Yorker*, 16 July 2001, pp. 32–8; Bill Owens [Adm., USN, Ret.] with Ed Offley, *Lifting the Fog of War* (New York: Farrar, Straus, Giroux, 2000). An argument for continuity, at least for ground warfare, is Stephen Biddle, "Assessing Theories of Future Warfare," in *The Use of Force after the Cold War*, ed. H. W. Brands (College Station: Texas A&M Univ. Press, 2001), pp. 217–88. For an overview, see Lawrence Freedman, *The Revolution in Strategic Affairs*, International Institute for Strategic Studies, Adelphi Paper 318 (Oxford, U.K.: Oxford Univ. Press, 1998).

20. Congress began pressing the Joint Chiefs of Staff and Department of Defense to consider the problem of overlapping roles and missions among the armed services as early as 1992. Congress formed a commission to address those issues in 1995, pressed for a

broader Quadrennial Defense Review (QDR) in 1997 (with a National Defense Panel to review and critique the effort immediately after), another QDR in 2001, and in 1998 urged the U.S. Commission on National Security/21st Century, to take an "end to end," or more comprehensive, look at national security and report in 2001. See Les Aspin, *Report on the Bottom-Up Review* (Washington, D.C.: Office of the Secretary of Defense, October 1993), on the World Wide Web at http://www.fas.org/man/docs/bur/index.html (5 October 2000); *Directions for Defense, Roles and Missions Commission of the Armed Forces: Report to Congress, the Secretary of Defense, and the Chairman of the Joint Chiefs of Staff*, 24 May 1995, executive summary, on the World Wide Web at http://www.fas.org/man/docs/corm95/di1062.html (26 November 2000); William S. Cohen, *Report of the Quadrennial Defense Review*, May 1997, on the World Wide Web at http://www.defenselink.mil/pubs/qdr/index.html (26 November 2000); Report of the National Defense Panel, December 1997, *Transforming Defense: National Security in the 21st Century*, on the World Wide Web at http://www.fas.org/man/docs/ndp/toc.htm (links from this table of contents) (2 August 2001); *Road Map for National Security: Imperative for Change: The Phase III Report of the U.S. Commission on National Security/21st Century, March 15, 2001* (n.p. [Washington]: n.p. [U.S. Commission on National Security/21st Century], 2001); Background on the Quadrennial Defense Review May 1997, H.R. 3230, *National Defense Authorization Act for Fiscal Year 1997*, Title IX, Subtitle B, Sec. 923, *Quadrennial Defense Review—Force Structure Review*, on the World Wide Web at http://www.comw.org/qdr/backgrd.html (26 November 2000). For background, see Lorna S. Jaffe, *The Development of the Base Force* (Washington, D.C.: Joint History Office, Office of the Chairman of the Joint Chiefs of Staff, July 1993); *National Security Strategy of the United States* (Washington, D.C.: White House, August 1991); Colin Powell, Les Aspin, "DOD Bottom-Up Review, September 1, 1993," Defense Department briefing, Federal Information Systems Corporation, Federal News Service, accessed through Academic Universe, s.v. "Bottom Up Review" (13 December 2000). For an insider's admission of paralysis on change

within the Pentagon and the failure of outside reform efforts, see Owens, *Lifting the Fog
of War*, pp. 32–42, 166–77, 207–19. Revealing reportage about the 1997 QDR is in
George Wilson, *This War Really Matters:
Inside the Fight for Defense Dollars* (Washington, D.C.: Congressional Quarterly
Press, 2000), chaps. 1–3.

21. As of 26 June 2001, some two-thirds of the
fifty major recommendations of the U.S.
Commission on National Security/21st Century "were being acted upon in some fashion
by the Administration or Congress." Memorandum, "Recommendations' Status," 26
June 2001, enclosed in Charles G. Boyd to the
author, 27 June 2001. The author was a member of the national security study group supporting the commission. The G. W. Bush
administration is at least rhetorically committed to change; see James Gerstenzang,
"Bush Offers New Vision of Military," *Los
Angeles Times*, 12 December 2001, p. 1.

22. The battle over transforming defense policy
during the first months of the Bush adminis-
tration in 2001 was covered extensively in the
press. See, for example, reports by Thomas E.
Ricks, *Washington Post*, 20, 25 May; 22 June;
14, 19, 25 July; 3, 7, 18, 31 August; 9 Decem-
ber 2001; by Al Kamen, *Washington Post*, 16
May 2001. Also reports by Elaine Grossman,
Inside the Pentagon, 31 May; 14 June; 5, 19, 26
July; 17 August 2001; Stan Crock, *Business
Week*, 2 July, 6 August 2001; James Dao,
Thom Shanker, Thomas L. Friedman, *New
York Times*, 3 June; 11, 13, 14, 19, 26, 30
July; 18 August; 2 September 2001; James
Kitfield, Sydney J. Freedberg, Jr., and George
C. Wilson, *National Journal*, 3 March, 9
June, 14 July, 3 November 2001; Bill Gertz,
Rowan Scarborough, *Washington Times*, 24
April; 25 May; 11, 29 June; 13 July; 30 Au-
gust 2001; Robert Holzer, *Defense News*,
4–10 June, 23–29 July 2001; Morton M.
Kondracke, *Roll Call*, 26 July 2001; Andrea
Stone, *USA Today*, 27 July 2001; by William
M. Arkin, washingtonpost.com, 4 June, 16
July 2001; by Pat Towell, *Congressional Quar-
terly Weekly*, 12 May, 21 July 2001; by
Eun-Kyung Kim, Lisa Burgess, *European
Stars and Stripes*, 24 May, 2 June 2001; by
Vago Muradian, Hunter Keeter, *Defense
Daily International*, 4 May 2001, and *Defense
Daily*, 11, 25 May 2001; and by Michael

Duffy, *Time*, 27 August 2001. Also, editorials
and opinion pieces in the *Washington Post*, 7
February, 27 August 2001; *Weekly Standard*,
14 May, 23 July 2001; *Los Angeles Times*, 24
May 2001; *New York Times*, 25 May, 13 July,
20 August 2001; *Washington Times*, 25 May,
10 June 2001; *London Financial Times*, 27
June, 31 July 2001; *Wall Street Journal*, 13
July; 1, 27 August 2001; *USA Today*, 18 July
2001; *Boston Globe*, 22 July 2001; *U.S. News
and World Report*, 13 August 2001; *Milwau-
kee Journal Sentinel*, 27, 28 August 2001; and
Newsweek, 3 September 2001. The first public
attacks on Rumsfeld's efforts by the services
came in a widely disseminated e-mail from
former Army chief of staff Gordon Sullivan,
head of the Association of the U.S. Army, on
5 May and from active-duty and retired naval
officers defending aircraft carriers (Captain
William Toti in the *Washington Times*, 23
April 2001; the Chief of Naval Operations,
Admiral Vernon Clark, quoted in *Inside the
Navy*, 4 June 2001; retired admiral Leighton
W. Smith, Jr., in *National Defense*, June
2001). For an analysis of the institutional bar-
riers to change, see Thomas Mahnken,
"Transforming the U.S. Armed Forces: Rhetoric or Reality?" *Naval War College Review*,
Summer 2001, pp. 81–9. "If we could achieve
a 15 percent transformation in 10 years, I
would consider that reasonable," Deputy Secretary of Defense Paul Wolfowitz admitted in
August 2001; "I do not think there is going to
be a single decision that will not be opposed
by someone." Tom Canahuate, "Total U.S.
Military Transformation in 10 Years Not Realis-
tic, Says Wolfowitz," DefenseNews.com, 16 August 2001. For the current direction of
"transformation," see Wolfowitz, keynote address, Fletcher Conference on "Focusing National Power," Washington, D.C., 14 November
2001, on the World Wide Web at http://
www.defenselink.mil/speeches/2001/s20011114-
depsecdef.html (1 December 2001).

23. See, for example, Paul Quinn-Judge, "Doubts
of Top Brass on the Use of Power Carry Great
Weight," *Boston Globe*, 20 April 1994, p. 12;
Donald H. Rumsfeld, "Transforming the Military," *Foreign Affairs*, May/June 2002,
pp. 20–32; Eliot A. Cohen, "A Tale of Two
Secretaries," *Foreign Affairs*, May/June 2002,
pp. 33–46; and Elaine M. Grossman, "Re-
formers Unimpressed by Rumsfeld Plan to

Overhaul Military Brass," *Inside the Pentagon,* 18 April 2002, p. 1.

24. My understanding of the Kosovo air campaign comes from Clark, *Waging Modern War;* Andrew J. Bacevich and Eliot A. Cohen, eds., *War over Kosovo: Politics and Strategy in a Global Age* (New York: Columbia Univ. Press, 2001); Halberstam, *War in a Time of Peace,* pp. 364ff.; Benjamin S. Lambeth, *NATO's Air War for Kosovo: A Strategic and Operational Assessment* (Santa Monica, Calif.: RAND Corporation, 2001); Michael Mandelbaum, "A Perfect Failure," *Foreign Affairs,* October 1999, pp. 2–8; and Daniel L. Byman and Matthew C. Waxman, "Kosovo and the Great Air Power Debate," and Barry R. Posen, "The War for Kosovo," both *International Security,* Spring 2000, pp. 5–84.

25. In 1998–99, the Triangle Institute for Security Studies "Project on the Gap between the Military and Civilian Society" compared the attitudes, opinions, values, and perspectives of elite officers on active duty and in the reserves with a sample of elite civilians in the United States, and with the mass public. The officer sample came from senior-year cadets and midshipmen at the service academies and in the Reserve Officers Training Corps, and from officers selected for in-residence attendance at staff and war colleges and for the Capstone Course (for new flag officers) at National Defense University, in Washington, D.C. Comparable samples of reserve and National Guard officers were also surveyed. The elite civilian sample was a random selection from *Who's Who in America* and similar biographical compilations. The general-public sample came from a telephone poll, using a portion of the survey's questions, conducted by Princeton Survey Research Associates. Information on the project and its methods can be found at http://www.poli.duke.civmil and in the introduction and conclusion in Peter D. Feaver and Richard H. Kohn, eds., *Soldiers and Civilians: The Civil-Military Gap and American National Security* (Cambridge, Mass.: MIT Press, 2001). The figures for military officers cited in this essay do not include students in precommissioning programs. In the survey, 49 percent of the active-duty military officers said they would leave military service "if the senior uniformed leadership does not stand up for what is right in military policy." This was the second most-listed choice of nine offered, exceeded only by "if the challenge and sense of fulfillment I derive from my service were less" (68 percent). (All percentages are rounded to the nearest whole number.) For a sense of the bitterness in the officer corps, particularly toward the senior uniformed leadership, see "Chief of Staff of the Army's Leadership Survey: Command and General Staff College Survey of 760 Mid-Career Students (Majors with a Few LTCs)," n.d. [Spring 2000], on the World Wide Web at http://www.d-n-i.net/FCS_Folder/leadership_comments.htm (30 November 2001); Ed Offley, "Young Officers' Anger, Frustration Stun Navy's Top Brass," *Seattle Post-Intelligencer,* 29 January 2000, on the World Wide Web at http://seattlep-i.nwsource.com/local/navy29.shtml (30 November 2001); Rowan Scarborough, "Army Colonels Reject Choice Assignments," *Washington Times,* 1 November 2000, p. A1; Paul Richter, "Glamour of America's Military Schools Fading for Youth," *Los Angeles Times,* 15 August 2000, p. 16; Justin P. D. Wilcox [Cpt., USA], "Military Experience Exposes 'Readiness Lie,'" *USA Today,* 5 September 2000, p. 26. Wilcox, a West Pointer, was leaving the service after five years because of underfunding, "more attention placed on landscaping and details . . . than on training," because "pursuit of mediocrity has become the norm," and for other reasons. "When," he asked, "will a general officer finally lay his stars on the table and stand up to the current administration for his soldiers?" One of the earlier attacks on the senior leadership was David H. Hackworth, "Too Much Brass, Too Little Brash," *Atlanta Constitution,* 2 March 1994, p. 11. For survey data and analysis, see *American Military Culture in the Twenty-first Century: A Report of the CSIS International Security Program* (Washington, D.C.: Center for Strategic and International Studies, 2000), pp. xxii, xxv, 17–8, 23–4, 45, 71–2. For an indication of a slippage in quality, see David S. C. Chu and John Brown, "Ensuring Quality People in Defense," in *Keeping the Edge: Managing Defense for the Future,* ed. Ashton B. Carter and John P. White (Cambridge, Mass.: MIT Press, 2001), p. 206. These events followed the downsizing of the armed services, which in the Army officer corps damaged morale, loosened

organizational commitment, and undermined professionalism. See David McCormick, *The Downsized Warrior: America's Army in Transition* (New York: New York Univ. Press, 1998), chap. 4, esp. pp. 127–9.

26. I am indebted to Alfred Goldberg, historian in the Office of the Secretary of Defense since 1973, for the insight about civilian control being situational. I used this definition first in "Out of Control: The Crisis in Civil-Military Relations," *National Interest*, Spring 1994, pp. 16–7. A similar definition, emphasizing the relative weight of military and civilian in decisions and decision making, is found in Michael Desch, *Civilian Control of the Military: The Changing Security Environment* (Baltimore: Johns Hopkins Univ. Press, 1999), esp. chaps. 1–3 and appendix. See also the discussion in Yehuda Ben Meir, *Civil-Military Relations in Israel* (New York: Columbia Univ. Press, 1995), chap. 2 ("Civilian Control"). In an important forthcoming work on civil-military relations, Peter Feaver distinguishes between trying to overthrow civilian authority (as in a coup) and simply shirking in carrying out the orders or wishes of the civilians. He explores the latter in depth, interpreting military subordination to civil authority as a variable rather than a given. See his *Armed Servants: Agency, Oversight, and Civilian Control* (Cambridge, Mass.: Harvard Univ. Press, in press).

27. See James R. Locher III, "Has It Worked? The Goldwater-Nichols Reorganization Act," *Naval War College Review*, Autumn 2001, pp. 108–9.

28. Pentagon reporter David Martin, in his "Landing the Eagle," *Vanity Fair*, November 1993, p. 153, described the Joint Staff this way: "Made up of 1,400 men and women, mostly in uniform, the Joint Staff analyzes the military consequences of the various options proposed by the administration. The answers they come up with can stop a fledgling policy dead in its tracks. You want to stop the bloodshed in Bosnia? Sure, we can do it. But it will take 500,000 troops and the second you pull them out the fighting will resume." For an indication of the Joint Staff's analytical (and political) advantages over the Office of the Secretary of Defense in the 2001 QDR, see Elaine Grossman, "Shelton Mulls Holding Key Civilian-Led Review to Exacting Standards," *Inside the Pentagon*, 2 August 2001,

p. 1. See also James Kitfield, "Pentagon Power Shift," *Government Executive*, April 1994, p. 72.

29. Owens, *Lifting the Fog of War*, pp. 172–4; John M. Shalikashvili et al., "Keeping the Edge in Joint Operations," in *Keeping the Edge*, ed. Carter and White, pp. 39–42, 44–5; Robert Holzer and Stephen C. LeSueur, "JCS Quietly Gathers Up Reins of Power," *Defense News*, 13–19 June 1994.

30. Conversation with an officer at a war college, June 1999. In late 2001, Secretary of Defense Donald Rumsfeld asked Congress's permission to reduce the various legislative liaison staffs in the Pentagon by almost half, to 250, because, as he reportedly believed, "some congressional liaison officers may be working at cross purposes with the Bush administration's plan by pushing their own agency or command instead of the Pentagon's top priorities." Rick Maze, "Senate Wants to Reduce Number of Military Liaisons," ArmyTimes.com, 4 December 2001.

31. Dana Priest, "The Proconsuls: Patrolling the World," in three front-page installments: "A Four-Star Foreign Policy?" "An Engagement in 10 Time Zones," and "CINCs Don't Swim with State," *Washington Post*, 28, 29, and 30 September 2000, respectively. See also the remarks of Dana Priest and Robert B. Oakley in the State Department Open Forum, 23 March 2001, and U.S. Secretary of State, "Civil Military Affairs and U.S. Diplomacy: The Changing Roles of the Regional Commanders-in-Chief," cable message to all diplomatic and consular posts, 1 July 2001. Writing from Paris, the journalist William Pfaff had highlighted the change a year earlier. "It is not too much to say that there is a distinct foreign policy of military inspiration, conducted from the Pentagon," he wrote, citing the conflicting messages sent by the American military to its Indonesian counterparts during the East Timor crisis. See "Beware of a Military Penchant for a Parallel Foreign Policy," *International Herald Tribune*, 22 September 1999, on the World Wide Web at http://www.iht.com/IHT/WP99/wp092299.html (5 December 2001). For an indication of how one regional commander actively sought to determine policy and influence diplomacy, in this case intervention to prevent ethnic cleansing in Kosovo, see Clark, *Waging War*, chaps. 5–6. Another regional commander,

Marine Corps general Anthony Zinni of U.S. Central Command, described himself as a "proconsul," hinting an analogy with a post in the ancient Roman republic and empire that mixed enormous political, military, and judicial powers over the population of a province. This author may have been the first to suggest that label to General Zinni, in an exchange at U.S. Central Command headquarters, Tampa, Florida, April 1998.

32. Andrew J. Bacevich, "Discord Still: Clinton and the Military," *Washington Post*, 3 January 1999, p. C01.

33. See the sources in note 22 above. An insightful summation is Michael Duffy, "Rumsfeld: Older but Wiser?" *Time*, 27 August 2001, pp. 22–7.

34. Wilson, *This War Really Matters*, takes a detailed, and particularly revealing, look at the "decision-making process for national defense" (p. 3) for the 1997–99 period, especially the interactions between the civilians in the executive branch, the Congress, and the Joint Chiefs. To understand the extent to which the armed services are expected to press their own institutional interests with Congress, see Stephen K. Scroggs, *Army Relations with Congress: Thick Armor, Dull Sword, Slow Horse* (Westport, Conn.: Praeger, 2000).

35. Lewis Sorley, *Thunderbolt: General Creighton Abrams and the Army of His Times* (New York: Simon and Schuster, 1992), pp. 361–4; Herbert Y. Schandler, *The Unmaking of a President: Lyndon Johnson and Vietnam* (Princeton, N.J.: Princeton Univ. Press, 1977), pp. 39, 56, 103, 305; and Eric Q. Winograd, "Officials: Homeland Defense Mission Will Mean Changes for the Guard," *Inside the Army*, 19 November 2001, p. 1. James Schlesinger, the secretary of defense who must have approved this change in force structure, confirmed this interpretation in the very process of questioning it: "This would not really be like Abe [Abrams]. He had the view that the military must defer to the civilians, even to an extraordinary degree. I speculate that the military sought to fix the incentives so that the civilians would act appropriately." Quoted in Duncan, *Citizen Warriors*, pp. 271–2.

36. William J. Crowe, Jr. [Adm., USN], *The Line of Fire: From Washington to the Gulf, the*

Politics and Battles of the New Military (New York: Simon and Schuster, 1993), pp. 41, 127, 152–9, 161, 177, 180–5, 189–90, 212–41, 304–5, 309, 312–9, 341–5; Bob Woodward, *The Commanders* (New York: Simon and Schuster, 1991), p. 40.

37. See, for example, Barton Gellman, "Rumblings of Discord Heard in Pentagon," *Washington Post*, 20 June 1993, p. A1.

38. J. G. Prout III, memorandum for the Commander in Chief, U.S. Pacific Fleet, "Subj: CNO Comments at Surface Warfare Flag Officer Conference (SWFOC)," 23 September 1994, copy in possession of the author.

39. *Directions for Defense*; Robert Holzer, "Experts: Streamlined Staff at OSD Could Save Billions," *Defense News*, 2–8 December 1996, p. 28.

40. For insight into the military's influence over the character of the intervention in Bosnia, see Ivo H. Daalder, *Getting to Dayton: The Making of America's Bosnia Policy* (Washington, D.C.: Brookings Institution Press, 2000), pp. 140–53, 173–8; Dan Blumenthal, "Clinton, the Military, and Bosnia, 1993–1995: A Study in Dysfunctional Civil Military Relations," Soldiers, Statesmen, and the Use of Force Seminar, Johns Hopkins School of Advanced International Studies, Washington, D.C., 7 June 1999; and Clark, *Waging War*, pp. 55–66, 73, 79–80. Clark, who was the senior U.S. military adviser at the Dayton negotiations, put it this way (p. 59): "Under our agreement, we were seeking to limit the obligations of the military . . . but to give the commander unlimited authority to accomplish these limited obligations." A background analysis is Susan L. Woodward, "Upside-Down Policy: The U.S. Debate on the Use of Force and the Case of Bosnia," in *Use of Force*, ed. Brands, pp. 111–34. In an analysis of civil-military conflicts between 1938 and 1997, Michael C. Desch argues that civilian control weakened in the United States during the 1990s. He finds that civilians prevailed in fifty-nine of sixty-two instances of civil-military conflict before the 1990s but in only five of twelve in that decade. See his *Civilian Control of the Military*, chap. 3 and appendix.

41. Charles G. Boyd, "America Prolongs the War in Bosnia," *New York Times*, 9 August 1995,

p. 19, and "Making Peace with the Guilty: The Truth about Bosnia," *Foreign Affairs*, October 1995, pp. 22–38. The op-ed began, "Having spent the last two years as deputy commander of the U.S. European Command, I have found that my views on the frustrating events in Bosnia differ from much of the conventional wisdom in Washington."

42. Bill Keller, "The World according to Powell," *New York Times Magazine*, 25 November 2001, p. 65.

43. For a fuller discussion of General Powell's efforts to circumvent civilian control, see Kohn, "Out of Control," pp. 8–13, and with Powell's reply, comments by John Lehman, William Odom, and Samuel P. Huntington, and my response in *National Interest*, Summer 1994, pp. 23–31. Other profiles and supporting material are in Jon Meacham, "How Colin Powell Plays the Game," *Washington Monthly*, December 1994, pp. 33–42; Charles Lane, "The Legend of Colin Powell," *New Republic*, 17 April 1995, pp. 20–32; Michael R. Gordon and Bernard E. Trainor, "Beltway Warrior," *New York Times Magazine*, 27 August 1995, pp. 40–3; Keller, "World according to Powell," pp. 61ff.; Michael C. Desch and Sharon K. Weiner, eds., *Colin Powell as JCS Chairman: A Panel Discussion on American Civil-Military Relations, October 23, 1995*, Project on U.S. Post–Cold War Civil-Military Relations, Working Paper 1 (Cambridge, Mass.: Harvard University, John M. Olin Institute for Strategic Studies, December 1995); Lawrence F. Kaplan, "Yesterday's Man: Colin Powell's Out-of-Date Foreign Policy," *New Republic*, 1 January 2001, pp. 17–21.

44. Eric Schmitt and Elaine Sciolino, "To Run Pentagon, Bush Sought Proven Manager with Muscle," *New York Times*, 1 January 2001, p. 1; Bill Gertz and Rowan Scarborough, "Inside the Ring," *Washington Times*, 26 January 2001, p. A9. Significantly, Powell's close friend Richard Armitage, who had been mentioned frequently for the position of deputy secretary of defense, was not offered that position and instead became deputy secretary of state.

45. T. Harry Williams, *Lincoln and His Generals* (New York: Random House, 1952), remains indispensable. See also Richard N. Current, *The Lincoln Nobody Knows* (New York: McGraw-Hill, 1958), p. 169; David Herbert Donald, *Lincoln* (New York: Simon and Schuster, 1995), pp. 386–8; and Bruce Tap, *Over Lincoln's Shoulder: The Committee on the Conduct of the War* (Lawrence: Univ. Press of Kansas, 1998), pp. 151–4.

46. Timothy D. Johnson, *Winfield Scott: The Quest for Military Glory* (Lawrence: Univ. Press of Kansas, 1998), pp. 217–9; John E. Marszalek, *Sherman: A Soldier's Passion for Order* (New York: Free Press, 1993), pp. 386–9.

47. Mark Russell Shulman, *Navalism and the Emergence of American Sea Power, 1882–1893* (Annapolis, Md.: Naval Institute Press, 1995), pp. 46–57, 152–3; Paul A. C. Koistinen, *Mobilizing for Modern War: The Political Economy of American Warfare, 1865–1919* (Lawrence: Univ. Press of Kansas, 1997), pp. 48–57; Benjamin Franklin Cooling, *Gray Steel and Blue Water Navy: The Formative Years of America's Military-Industrial Complex, 1881–1917* (Hamden, Conn.: Archon Books, 1979), chaps. 3–4, postscript. See also Kurt Hackemer, *The U.S. Navy and the Origins of the Military-Industrial Complex, 1847–1883* (Annapolis, Md.: Naval Institute Press, 2001), and his "Building the Military-Industrial Relationship: The U.S. Navy and American Business, 1854–1883," *Naval War College Review*, Spring 1999, pp. 89–111.

48. DeWitt S. Copp, *A Few Great Captains: The Men and Events That Shaped the Development of U.S. Air Power* (Garden City, N.Y.: Doubleday, 1980); David E. Johnson, *Fast Tanks and Heavy Bombers: Innovation in the U.S. Army, 1917–1945* (Ithaca, N.Y.: Cornell Univ. Press, 1998), pp. 66–9, 81–4, 86–90, 102–3, 158–60, 220–2, 227–8; Randall R. Rice, "The Politics of Air Power: From Confrontation to Cooperation in Army Aviation Civil-Military Relations, 1919–1940" (dissertation, University of North Carolina at Chapel Hill, 2002).

49. Quoted in Marriner Eccles, *Beckoning Frontiers: Public and Personal Recollections*, ed. Sidney Hyman (New York: Knopf, 1951), p. 336. For a sense of Theodore Roosevelt's troubles with the services, see his letters to Elihu Root, 7 March 1902; to Oswald Garrison Villard, 22 March 1902; to Leonard Wood, 4 June 1904; and to Truman H. Newberry, 28 August 1908, quoted in Elting E. Morison, ed., *The Letters of Theodore Roosevelt*, 8 vols. (Cambridge, Mass.: Harvard

Univ. Press, 1951–54), vol. 3, pp. 241, 247; vol. 4, p. 820; vol. 6, p. 1199. See also the forthcoming study of Roosevelt as commander in chief by Matthew M. Oyos, who supplied excerpts from the above documents; and Oyos, "Theodore Roosevelt, Congress, and the Military: U.S. Civil-Military Relations in the Early Twentieth Century," *Presidential Studies Quarterly*, vol. 30, 2000, pp. 312–30.

50. The civil-military battles of the 1940s, 1950s, and 1960s are covered in a number of works, among them: Demetrios Caraley, *The Politics of Military Unification: A Study of Conflict and the Policy Process* (New York: Columbia Univ. Press, 1966); Herman S. Wolk, *The Struggle for Air Force Independence, 1943–1947* (Washington, D.C.: Air Force History and Museums Program, 1997); Jeffrey G. Barlow, *Revolt of the Admirals: The Fight for Naval Aviation, 1945–1950* (Washington, D.C.: Naval Historical Center, 1994); Steven L. Rearden, *The Formative Years, 1947–1950,* vol. 1 of *History of the Office of the Secretary of Defense* (Washington, D.C.: Historical Office, Office of the Secretary of Defense, 1984); Robert L. Watson, *Into the Missile Age, 1956–1960,* vol. 4 of *History of the Office of the Secretary of Defense* (Washington, D.C.: Historical Office, Office of the Secretary of Defense, 1997); Andrew J. Bacevich, "Generals versus the President: Eisenhower and the Army, 1953–1955," in *Security in a Changing World: Case Studies in U.S. National Security Management,* ed. Volker C. Franke (Westport, Conn.: Praeger, 2002), pp. 83–99; and Deborah Shapley, *Promise and Power: The Life and Times of Robert McNamara* (Boston: Little, Brown, 1993).

51. For a brief history of civilian control, see Richard H. Kohn, "Civil-Military Relations: Civilian Control of the Military," in *The Oxford Companion to American Military History,* ed. John Whiteclay Chambers II (New York: Oxford Univ. Press, 1999), pp. 122–5. Similar interpretations of the conflict inherent in the relationship are Russell F. Weigley, "The American Military and the Principle of Civilian Control from McClellan to Powell," *Journal of Military History,* special issue, vol. 57, 1993, pp. 27–59; Russell F. Weigley, "The American Civil-Military Cultural Gap: A Historical Perspective, Colonial Times to the Present," in *Soldiers and Civilians,* ed. Feaver

and Kohn, chap. 5; Ronald H. Spector, "Operation Who Says: Tension between Civilian and Military Leaders Is Inevitable," *Washington Post,* 22 August 1999, p. B1; and Peter D. Feaver, "Discord and Divisions of Labor: The Evolution of Civil-Military Conflict in the United States," paper presented at the annual meeting of the American Political Science Association, Washington, D.C., 1993. A particularly cogent analysis from a generation ago, by a scholar who both studied the issues and participated as a senior civilian official in the Pentagon, is Adam Yarmolinsky, "Civilian Control: New Perspectives for New Problems," *Indiana Law Journal,* vol. 49, 1974, pp. 654–71.

52. See, for example, Dana Priest, "Mine Decision Boosts Clinton-Military Relations," *Washington Post,* 21 September 1997, p. A22; Ernest Blazar, "Inside the Ring," *Washington Times,* 8 June 1998, p. 11; Jonathan S. Landay, "U.S. Losing Handle on Its Diplomacy in a Kosovo 'at War,'" *Christian Science Monitor,* 5 June 1998, p. 7; Daniel Rearick, "An Unfortunate Opposition: U.S. Policy toward the Establishment of the International Criminal Court" (honors thesis, University of North Carolina at Chapel Hill, 2000).

53. In *The Clustered World: How We Live, What We Buy, and What It All Means about Who We Are* (Boston: Little, Brown, 2000), a study of consumerism and lifestyles, Michael J. Weiss identifies the military as one of "sixty-two distinct population groups each with its own set of values, culture and means of coping with today's problems" (p. 11). His thesis is that the country has become splintered and fragmented (see pp. 258–9 and chap. 1). For the military's "presence" in American society, see the late Adam Yarmolinsky's comprehensive *The Military Establishment: Its Impacts on American Society* (New York: Harper and Row, 1971), and James Burk, "The Military's Presence in American Society," in *Soldiers and Civilians,* ed. Feaver and Kohn, chap. 6. In 1985, "a group of 31 military and veterans organizations that lobby for the uniformed services on personnel and pay issues" representing some "6 million veterans and their families" banded together to form the "Military Coalition," a force that in the opinion of one thoughtful retired general is "potentially far

more numerous and powerful than the NRA!!!" Stephen Barr, "Military Pay Expert Retires," *Washington Post*, 12 March 2001, p. B2; Ted Metaxis e-mail to the author, 24 October 1999.

54. Donald Rumsfeld, "Rumsfeld's Rules," rev. ed., January 17, 2001, on the World Wide Web at http://www.defenselink.mil/news/jan2001/rumsfeldsrules.pdf (29 January 2001).

55. Department of Defense, *Quadrennial Defense Review Report*, 30 September 2001, on the World Wide Web at http://www.defenselink.mil/pubs/qdr2001.pdf (6 October 2001); Anne Plummer, "Pentagon Launches Some 50 Reviews in Major Defense Planning Effort," *Inside the Pentagon*, 15 November 2001, p. 1; John Liang, "Rumsfeld Supports Switching Future QDRs to Administration's Second Year," InsideDefense.com, 6 December 2001.

56. Thomas E. Ricks, "Target Approval Delays Cost Air Force Key Hits," *Washington Post*, 18 November 2001, p. 1, and "Rumsfeld's Hands-On War: Afghan Campaign Shaped by Secretary's Views, Personality," *Washington Post*, 19 December 2001, p. 1; Esther Schrader, "Action Role a Better Fit for Rumsfeld," *Los Angeles Times*, 11 November 2001, p. 22; Lawrence F. Kaplan, "Ours to Lose: Why Is Bush Repeating Clinton's Mistakes?" *New Republic*, 12 November 2001, pp. 25–6; Robert Kagan and William Kristol, "Getting Serious," *Weekly Standard*, 19 November 2001, pp. 7–8; J. Michael Waller, "Rumsfeld: Plagues of Biblical Job," *Insight Magazine*, 10 December 2001; Damian Whitworth and Roland Watson, "Rumsfeld at Odds with His Generals," *London Times*, 16 October 2001, p. 5; Toby Harnden, "Rumsfeld Calls for End to Old Tactics of War," *London Daily Telegraph*, 16 October 2001, p. 8.

57. Quoted in Donald Smythe, *Guerrilla Warrior: The Early Life of John J. Pershing* (New York: Scribner's, 1973), p. 278.

58. Omar N. Bradley, *A Soldier's Story* (New York: Henry Holt, 1951), p. 147. For an outline of the four factors underlying civilian control in the United States historically, see my "Civilian Control of the Military," pp. 122–5.

59. The Gallup polling organization has surveyed Americans annually on their confidence in major institutions since the early 1970s, and the military has topped the list since 1987, with over 60 percent expressing a "great deal" or "quite a lot" of confidence. See Frank Newport, "Military Retains Top Position in Americans' Confidence Ratings," 25 June 2001, on the World Wide Web at http://www.gallup.com/poll/releases/pr010625.asp (2 December 2001) and "Small Business and Military Generate Most Confidence in Americans," 15 August 1997, on the World Wide Web at http://www.gallup.com/poll/releases/ pr970815.asp (2 December 2001); "Gallup Poll Topics: A-Z: Confidence in Institutions," 8–10 June 2001, on the World Wide Web at http://www.gallup.com/poll/indicators/indconfidence.asp (2 December 2001). For excellent analyses of the change in public attitudes toward the military since the late 1960s, see David C. King and Zachary Karabell, "The Generation of Trust: Public Confidence in the U.S. Military since Vietnam," revision of a paper presented to the Duke University political science department, 29 January 1999, to be published in 2002 by the American Enterprise Institute; and Richard Sobel, "The Authoritarian Reflex and Public Support for the U.S. Military: An Anomaly?" paper presented at the annual meeting of the Midwest Political Science Association, 16 April 1999. Respect for lawyers is low and has been declining in recent years. See Darren K. Carlson, "Nurses Remain at Top of Honest and Ethics Poll," 27 November 2000, on the World Wide Web at http://www.gallup.com/poll/releases/Pr001127.asp (2 December 2001).

60. Joseph S. Nye, Jr., Philip D. Zelikow, and David C. King, eds., *Why People Don't Trust Government* (Cambridge, Mass.: Harvard Univ. Press, 1997); Albert H. Cantril and Susan Davis Cantril, *Reading Mixed Signals: Ambivalence in American Public Opinion about Government* (Washington, D.C.: Woodrow Wilson Center Press, 1999). The decline in trust of government and confidence in public institutions has not been limited to the United States. See Susan J. Pharr and Robert D. Putnam, eds., *Disaffected Democracies: What's Troubling the Trilateral Countries?* (Princeton, N.J.: Princeton Univ. Press, 2000). Trust in government in the United States after the 11 September attacks jumped dramatically to the highest level since

1968. Frank Newport, "Trust in Government Increases Sharply in Wake of Terrorist Attacks," 12 October 2001, on the World Wide Web at http://www.gallup.com/poll/releases/pr011012.asp (2 December 2001); Alexander Stille, "Suddenly, Americans Trust Uncle Sam," *New York Times*, 3 November, p. A11; and John D. Donahue, "Is Government the Good Guy?" *New York Times*, 13 December 2001, p. A31. Whether the attacks will reverse the long-term trend remains to be seen.

61. For critiques of journalism in general and coverage of the military in particular, see Bill Kovach and Tom Rosenstiel, *Warp Speed: America in the Age of Mixed Media* (New York: Century Foundation Press, 1999); Scott Shuger, "First, the Bad News: The Big Daily Newspapers Get Some Things Right. National Defense Isn't One of Them," *Mother Jones*, September/October 1998, pp. 72–6. My views come from a decade of close reading of reporting on national security issues. An example of lack of interest in civil-military relations is the absence in the media of reaction to and interpretation of the detailed and persuasive reports of Dana Priest (see note 31 above) about the growth in power of the regional commanders, discussed previously. Typical of press misunderstanding is the editorial "Unifying Armed Forces Requires Radical Change" in the 18 June 2001 *Honolulu Star-Bulletin,* calling for abolition of the separate military departments, replacement of the JCS by a "single Chief of Military Staff who would command the armed forces," and further empowerment of the regional commanders. The editorial purports to "make the Secretary of Defense a genuine master of the Pentagon rather than a referee among warring factions," but the recommendations would destroy a secretary's ability to monitor and supervise one of the world's largest, and most complex, bureaucratic structures.

62. See William J. Bennett, *The Index of Leading Cultural Indicators: American Society at the End of the Twentieth Century*, updated and expanded ed. (New York: Broadway Books, 1999); Marc Miringoff and Marque-Luisa Miringoff, *The Social Health of the Nation: How America Is Really Doing* (New York: Oxford Univ. Press, 1999); James H. Billington, "The Human Consequences of the Information Revolution," Ditchley Foundation Lecture 37 (Chipping Norton, U.K.: Ditchley Foundation, 2000); Robert D. Putnam, *Bowling Alone: The Collapse and Revival of American Community* (New York: Simon and Schuster, 2000); Everett Carl Ladd, *The Ladd Report* (New York: Free Press, 1999); Weiss, *The Clustered World,* pp. 10–1, 14–5, 19–25, 43–4; Theda Skocpol and Morris P. Fiorina, eds., *Civic Engagement in American Democracy* (Washington, D.C.: Brookings Institution Press, 1999), essays 1, 12, 13; Derek Bok, *The Trouble with Government* (Cambridge, Mass.: Harvard Univ. Press, 2001), pp. 386–98; William Chaloupka, *Everybody Knows: Cynicism in America* (Minneapolis: Univ. of Minnesota Press, 1999); Robert D. Kaplan, *An Empire Wilderness: Travels into America's Future* (New York: Random House, 1998); and Adam B. Seligman, *The Problem of Trust* (Princeton, N.J.: Princeton Univ. Press, 1997). More hopeful though still cautious pictures are Robert William Fogel, *The Fourth Great Awakening & the Future of Egalitarianism* (Chicago: Univ. of Chicago Press, 2000); and Francis Fukuyama, *The Great Disruption: Human Nature and the Reconstitution of Social Order* (New York: Free Press, 1999).

63. In the TISS survey, a number of the 250-some questions examined attitudes about the proper role of the military in society. For example, 49 percent of elite civilians and 68 percent of the mass public agreed ("strongly" or "somewhat") that "in wartime, civilian government leaders should let the military take over running the war," a position echoed by even as distinguished a scholar as Amitai Etzioni ("How Not to Win the War," *USA Today,* 7 November 2001, p. 15). To the question, "Members of the military should be allowed to publicly express their political views just like any other citizen," 59 percent of the civilian elite and 84 percent of the general public agreed. Civilians were much more likely than the military to condone leaking documents to the press in various situations. The distinguished sociologist James A. Davis felt the results "make one's hair stand on end" but suggested as a "simple explanation" that they are accounted for by "cynicism about civilian politics," Americans' high regard for "their military," and by the ideas that civilian control is "a fairly sophisticated doctrine, while common sense suggests that important decisions

should be made by people who are best in-
formed." See his "Attitudes and Opinions
among Senior Military Officers and a U.S.
Cross-Section, 1998–1999," in *Soldiers and
Civilians*, ed. Feaver and Kohn, p. 120 and
esp. table 2.10. My point is that whatever the
explanation, the very positive image of the
military held by Americans in the last dozen
or so years diverges considerably from what
seems to have been the historical norm. See
C. Robert Kemble, *The Image of the Army Officer in America: Background for Current
Views* (Westport, Conn.: Greenwood, 1973);
Samuel P. Huntington, *The Soldier and the
State: The Theory and Politics of Civil-Military
Relations* (Cambridge, Mass.: Harvard Univ.
Press, 1957), particularly part 2. At the same
time, 47 percent of the general public did *not*
think "civilian control of the military is abso-
lutely safe and secure in the United States,"
and 68 percent thought that "if civilian leaders order the military to do something that it
opposes, military leaders will seek ways to
avoid carrying out the order" at least "some
of the time" (30 percent thought "all" or
"most of the time"). For the decline in civics
education and understanding, see Chris
Hedges, "35% of High School Seniors Fail
National Civics Test," *New York Times*, 21
November 1999, p. 17; Bok, *Trouble with
Government*, pp. 403–6.

64. For the caricatures in popular literature and
films, see Howard Harper, "The Military and
Society: Reaching and Reflecting Audiences in
Fiction and Film," *Armed Forces & Society*, vol.
27, 2001, pp. 231–48. Charles C. Moskos, "Toward a Postmodern Military: The United
States as a Paradigm," in *The Postmodern Military: Armed Forces after the Cold War*, ed.
Charles C. Moskos, John Allen Williams, and
David R. Segal (New York: Oxford Univ. Press,
2000), p. 20; Moskos, "What Ails the All-
Volunteer Force: An Institutional Perspective,"
Parameters, Summer 2001, pp. 34–5; and "Interview: James Webb," U.S. Naval Institute *Proceedings*, April 2000, pp. 78–9, all argue that the
military is pictured negatively in film. But King
and Karabell, "Generation of Trust," pp. 6–7,
judge that current portrayals are the most
"positive . . . since World War II."

65. Gary Hart, *The Minuteman: Restoring an
Army of the People* (New York: Free Press,
1998), particularly chaps. 1, 3.

66. In the TISS survey of "elite" officers, some 40
percent of the National Guard and 25 percent
of the reserve respondents listed their occupation as "military," which suggests that they
are in uniform full-time or work somewhere
in national defense, either for government or
industry. See David Paul Filer, "Military Reserves: Bridging the Culture Gap between Civilian Society and the United States Military"
(M.A. thesis, Duke University, Durham,
North Carolina, 2001), pp. 46–7. In the fiscal
year 2001 defense authorization act, 6.6 percent of the Army National Guard and 20.6
percent of the Air National Guard were au-
thorized to be "dual status" civilian techni-
cians and uniformed members. Charlie Price
(National Guard Bureau of Public Affairs)
e-mail to author, 12 February 2001.

67. The similarity "attitudinally" between active-
duty officers and the National Guard and reserves on some of the questions in the TISS survey is addressed in Filer, "Military Reserves."
Other congruence is evident in the data.

68. See, for example, Jack Kelly, "U.S. Reliance
on Guards, Reservists Escalating," *Pittsburgh
Post-Gazette*, 28 October 2000, p. 9; Steven
Lee Myers, "Army Will Give National Guard
the Entire U.S. Role in Bosnia," *New York
Times*, 5 December 2000, p. A8; Winograd,
"Officials: Homeland Defense Mission Will
Mean Changes for the Guard," p. 1; David T.
Fautua, "Army Citizen-Soldiers: Active,
Guard, and Reserve Leaders Remain Silent
about Overuse of Reserve Components,"
Armed Forces Journal International, September 2000, pp. 72–4; John J. Miller, "Unre-
served: The Misuse of America's Reserve
Forces," *National Review*, 23 July 2001,
pp. 26ff.; and Duncan, *Citizen Warriors*,
pp. 214–7 and n. 25. Duncan calls the 1995
deployment of Guardsmen and reserves to
the Sinai for six months of peacekeeping duty
"unprecedented." See also Peter Bacqué,
"Guard Troops Will Head for Sinai in '95,"
Richmond Times-Dispatch, 28 January 1994,
p. B6. The reserve-component contribution
to active-duty missions has risen from about
one million man-days in 1986 to approxi-
mately thirteen million in each of the years
1996, 1997, and 1998. CSIS, *American Military Culture*, p. 19. See also Conrad C. Crane,
*Landpower and Crises: Army Roles and Mis-
sions in Smaller-Scale Contingencies during the*

1990s (Carlisle, Penna.: U.S. Army Strategic Studies Institute, January 2001), pp. 29–30.

69. Personal exchange, panel discussion on civil-military relations, Marine Corps Staff College, Quantico, Virginia, September 1998; personal exchange, lecture/discussion with twenty-six state adjutant generals, U.S. Army War College, Carlisle, Pennsylvania, October 1998.

70. The decline in citizen-soldiering and some of its implications are addressed in Andrew J. Bacevich, "Losing Private Ryan: Why the Citizen-Soldier Is MIA," *National Review*, 9 August 1999, pp. 32–4. Also Elliott Abrams and Andrew J. Bacevich, "A Symposium on Citizenship and Military Service"; Eliot A. Cohen, "Twilight of the Citizen-Soldier"; and James Burk, "The Military Obligation of Citizens since Vietnam"; all *Parameters*, Summer 2001, pp. 18–20, 23–8, 48–60, respectively. Also Hart, *Minuteman*, esp. pp. 16–7, 21–5. For a recent review of the end of conscription, see David R. Sands, "Military Draft Now Part of Past: Spain and Italy are the Latest European Nations to Abandon Compulsory Service," and "U.S. Talk of a Draft Probably Hot Air," *Washington Times*, 31 December 2000, pp. 1, 4, respectively.

71. In the TISS survey, well over 90 percent of the civilian elite said that the people they came into contact with "in the social or community groups to which [they] belong" were either "all civilians" or "mostly civilians with some military." The same was true (over 90 percent of respondents) in the workplace. Americans (both elite and general public) who have not served in the military also have fewer close friends who now serve or are veterans. The prospects for diminished civilian contact with, understanding of, and support for the military are analyzed in Paul Gronke and Peter D. Feaver, "Uncertain Confidence: Civilian and Military Attitudes about Civil-Military Relations," in *Soldiers and Civilians*, ed. Feaver and Kohn, chap. 3. Congressman Ike Skelton, ranking Democrat on the House Armed Services Committee, had already discerned the trend and its implications for support of the military; see Rasheeda Crayton, "Skelton Calls for More Military Support," *Kansas City Star*, 12 November 1997, p. 15. A more general comment comes from Brent Scowcroft, national security

adviser to Presidents Gerald Ford and George H. W. Bush: "With the lessened contact between the American people and the military, . . . the results will not be healthy." Scowcroft, "Judgment and Experience: George Bush's Foreign Policy," in *Presidential Judgment: Foreign Policy Decision Making in the White House*, ed. Aaron Lobel (Hollis, N.H.: Hollis, 2001), 115. The declining propensity of youth to serve is noted in Thomas W. Lippman, "With a Draft Cut Off, Nation's Society Climate Changed Sharply," *Washington Post*, 8 September 1998, p. 13. Lippman cites Pentagon "Youth Attitude Tracking Survey" figures indicating that some 32 percent of youth "expressed some desire to join the military" in 1973, the last year of the Cold War draft, but that by 1993 the figure had dropped to 25 percent and by 1997 to 12 percent. See also Moskos, "What Ails the All-Volunteer Force," pp. 39–41.

72. William T. Bianco and Jamie Markham, "Vanishing Veterans: The Decline of Military Experience in the U.S. Congress," in *Soldiers and Civilians*, ed. Feaver and Kohn, chap. 7.

73. Norman Ornstein, "The Legacy of Campaign 2000," *Washington Quarterly*, Spring 2001, p. 102; William M. Welch, "Most U.S. Lawmakers Lack Combat Experience," *USA Today*, 12 November 2001, p. 12. Writing before 11 September, Ornstein calls the present "Congress . . . clearly and irrevocably a post–Cold War Congress. Eighty-three percent, or 363 members, of the House were first elected in the 1990s, since the Berlin Wall fell, along with 57 members of the Senate. Few of these lawmakers, in either party, have an abiding interest in the U.S. role in the world. International issues are simply not high on their priority list." He notes also that in a typical post–World War II Congress, some three-quarters of the senators and more than half the representatives were veterans. Importantly, the newer veterans in Congress are quite likely to be Republicans, whereas in the past veterans were more or less evenly split. Donald N. Zillman, "Maintaining the Political Neutrality of the Military," *IUS* [Inter-University Seminar on Armed Forces and Society] *Newsletter*, Spring 2001, p. 17. In 2000, a retired rear admiral "started a 'National Defense P[olitical]A[ction]C[ommittee]' to support congressional candidates who have served in

the armed forces." "Inside Washington, D.C.: G.I. Joes and G.I. Janes Ready Their PAC," *National Journal*, 9 September 2000, p. 2759.

74. According to the newsletter of the Federal Voting Assistance Program, the military began voting in greater percentages than the public in 1984, and in 1996 "at an overall rate of 64%, compared to the 49% rate generated by the general public. The Uniformed Services' high participation rate can be directly attributed to the active voter assistance programs conducted by Service Commanders and to assistance from the state and local election officials in simplifying the absentee voting process and accommodating the special needs of the Uniformed Services." See "Military Retains High Participation Rates," *Voting Information News*, July 1997, p. 1. In the 1980 election, military voting was below civilian (49.7 to 52.6 percent). In the 1992 election, the Defense Department expanded the program, according to a reporter, "to register and turn out military voters," changing the "emphasis . . . from ensuring availability of voting forms to mustering ballots at the polls." Setting "for the first time . . . a target rate for participation," this "new focus on voter turnout . . . has led some Democratic and some independent analysts to suspect the Bush administration is trying to energize a predictably sympathetic voter base." Barton Gellman, "Pentagon Intensifies Effort to Muster Military Voters," *Washington Post*, 17 September 1992, p. A1. See also Daniel A. Gibran, *Absentee Voting: A Brief History of Suffrage Expansion in the United States* (Washington, D.C.: Federal Voting Assistance Program, August 2001).

75. Ole R. Holsti, "A Widening Gap between the U.S. Military and Civilian Society? Some Evidence, 1976–1996," *International Security*, Winter 1998/1999, p. 11; TISS survey data. Some observers think the actual Republican figure is much higher, many officers being reluctant to reveal a preference, "knowing full and well what the reaction would be if the percentage of Republicans in the elite military ranks was seen to approach 85 to 90 per cent, which I am told is a reasonable figure." This well-connected West Point graduate continued, "We're in danger of developing our own in-house Soviet-style military, one in which if you're not in 'the party,' you don't get ahead. I have spoken with several . . . who were run out of the Army near the beginning of their careers when commanders became aware that they had voted for Clinton in 1992. I have no doubt they are telling me the truth, and . . . I've spoken with some . . . who confirm their stories." Enclosure in Tom Ricks to the author, 20 November 2000. Generals and admirals—who, as older, more senior, and more experienced officers could be expected to be imbued with the more traditional ethic of nonaffiliation—have a slightly higher independent or nonpartisan self-identification. In 1984, *Newsweek* (9 July, p. 37) surveyed 257 flag officers, about a quarter of those on active duty; the results were Republican 52 percent, Democrat 4 percent, independent 43 percent, "don't know" 1 percent. Holsti's 1984 officer sample contained 29 percent independents. The TISS survey included seventy-four one and two-star officers: Republican 57 percent; Democrat 9 percent; independent, no preference, and other 34 percent. The TISS active-duty sample was 28 percent independent/no preference/other.

76. Pat Towell, "GOP Advertises Differences with Commander in Chief in Military-Oriented Papers," *Congressional Quarterly Weekly*, 11 December 1999, p. 2984; Republican National Committee advertisement, "Keeping the Commitment: Republicans Reverse Years of Military Neglect," *Air Force Times*, 13 December 1999, p. 57; Republican National Committee postcard to University of North Carolina Army ROTC cadre members, n.d. [fall 2000], in possession of author; Frank Abbott to author, 11 October 2000; David Wood, "Military Breaks Ranks with Non-Partisan Tradition," *Cleveland Plain Dealer*, 22 October 2000, p. 16. Just prior to the election, the Republican National Committee paid for e-mail messages from Colin Powell urging recipients to vote for "our Republican team"; Powell to Alvin Bernstein, subject "A Message from Colin L. Powell," 6 November 2000, in possession of author. In the 2000 election, about 72 percent of *overseas* military personnel, targeted particularly by Republicans, voted. The overall voting rate for the civilian population was 50 percent. Robert Suro, "Pentagon Will Revise Military Voting Procedures," *Washington Post*, 23 June 2001, p. 2. The Bush campaign pushed to count overseas military ballots, even questionable ones, in

counties where Bush was strong and to dis-
qualify those in counties where Gore was
strong, nearly resulting in a large enough net
gain to swing the outcome by itself. David
Barstow and Don Van Natta, Jr., "How Bush
Took Florida: Mining the Overseas Absentee
Vote," *New York Times*, 15 July 2001, p. 1.

77. Christopher McKee, *A Gentlemanly and Hon-
orable Profession: The Creation of the U.S. Na-
val Officer Corps, 1794–1815* (Annapolis, Md.:
Naval Institute Press, 1991), pp. 107–8; Wil-
liam B. Skelton, *An American Profession of
Arms: The Army Officer Corps, 1784–1861*
(Lawrence: Univ. Press of Kansas, 1992),
chap. 15; Edward M. Coffman, *The Old
Army: A Portrait of the American Army in
Peacetime, 1784–1898* (New York: Oxford
Univ. Press, 1986), pp. 87–96, 242–3, 266–9;
Peter Karsten, *The Naval Aristocracy: The
Golden Age of Annapolis and the Emergence of
Modern American Navalism* (New York: Free
Press, 1972), pp. 203–13.

78. General Lucian K. Truscott, Jr., in *The Twilight of the U.S. Cavalry: Life in the Old Army,
1917–1942* (Lawrence: Univ. Press of Kansas,
1989), remembers that "there was never
much partisan political feeling on military
posts, even during years of presidential elections. . . . [T]he military were isolated from
the political rivalries. . . . Then too, Regular
Army officers were sworn to uphold and defend the Constitution . . . and . . . carried out
orders regardless of the political party in
power. . . . Further, few officers maintained
voting residence, and absentee voting was rel-
atively rare at this time" (p. 130). Edward M.
Coffman, who has spent over two decades
studying the peacetime Army (his volume
covering the social history of the Army,
1898–1941, to follow his *The Old Army*, is
near completion), found that regular officers
in the nineteenth century "generally stayed
out of politics with rare exceptions" and during "the 20th century" had "virtually no participation in voting. For one thing, the
absentee ballot was not in vogue—and then
there was the problem of establishing residency but, as I picked up in interviews
[Coffman has done several hundred with veterans of the 1900–40 era], they didn't think it
was their place to vote. Again and again, both
officers and their wives told me that they
didn't vote until after retirement." Coffman

e-mail to the author, 23 July 1999. Non-
partisanship and lack of voting in the 1930s is
confirmed by Daniel Blumenthal in "Legal
Prescriptions, Customary Restrictions, Institutional Traditions: The Political Attitudes of
American Officers Leading Up to World War
II," seminar paper, National Security Law
Course, Duke University Law School, 4 April
1998.

79. I agree with Lance Betros, "Political Partisanship and the Military Ethic in America,"
Armed Forces & Society, vol. 27, 2001,
pp. 501–23, that the mere act of voting is not
partisan, but I think that continual voting
over time for the same party can lead to partisanship that *does* harm military professionalism. In a March 1999 discussion at the Naval
War College, Admiral Stanley Arthur felt that
officers who are sincere about their votes
"take ownership" of them, a commitment
that could undermine their ability to be neutral, apolitical instruments of the state. I do
not find that promoting one's armed service,
writing about national defense issues to affect
policy, and making alliances with politicians
to advance one's own personal and service interests are the same as the partisanship of
identifying personally with the ideology and
political and cultural agendas of a political
party, which is the kind of partisanship that
has emerged in the last two decades. For a
different view, see Betros, "Officer Professionalism in the Late Progressive Era," in *The
Future of Army Professionalism*, ed. Don
Snider and Gayle Watkins (New York:
McGraw-Hill, 2002).

80. Mackubin Thomas Owens, "The Democratic
Party's War on the Military," *Wall Street Jour-
nal*, 22 November 2000, p. 22. See also Tom
Donnelly, "Why Soldiers Dislike Democrats,"
Weekly Standard, 4 December 2000, p. 14.

81. Ed Offley, "Rejected Military Votes Spark
New Furor in Florida Election Count," *Stars
and Stripes Omnimedia*, 20 November 2000;
Thomas E. Ricks, "Democratic Ballot Challenges Anger Military," *Washington Post*, 21
November 2000, p. A18; Kenneth Allard,
"Military Ballot Mischief," *Washington Times*,
27 November 2000; Elaine M. Grossman,
"Rift over Florida Military Ballots Might Affect a Gore Administration," *Inside the Pentagon*, 30 November 2000, p. 1.

82. Triangle Institute for Security Studies, "Survey on the Military in the Post Cold War Era," 1999. The question read: "If civilian leaders order the military to do something that it opposes, military leaders will seek ways to avoid carrying out the order: all of the time [9 percent chose this answer]; most of the time [21 percent]; some of the time [38 percent]; rarely [20 percent]; never [8 percent]; no opinion [4 percent]." The telephone survey of over a thousand people was administered by Princeton Survey Research Associates in September 1998.

83. I made this argument more fully in "The Political Trap for the Military," *Raleigh (North Carolina) News & Observer*, 22 September 2000, p. A19, orig. pub. *Washington Post*, 19 September 2000, p. A23. See also Charles A. Stevenson, "Bridging the Gap between Warriors and Politicians," paper presented at the annual meeting of the American Political Science Association, Atlanta, Georgia, 2–5 September 1999.

84. Richard Holbrooke, *To End a War* (New York: Random House, 1998), pp. 144–6, 361–2. An indication of the bitterness that developed between Holbrooke and Admiral Leighton W. Smith, Commander in Chief, Allied Forces Southern Europe, who carried out the bombing on behalf of Nato's governing body, is in "Frontline: Give War a Chance," WGBH Educational Foundation, 2000, aired 11 May 1999, Public Broadcasting System. For a dispassionate view of the misunderstanding between political and military officials, see "Summary," in *Deliberate Force: A Case Study in Effective Bombing*, ed. Robert C. Owen [Col., USAF] (Maxwell Air Force Base [hereafter AFB], Ala.: Air Univ. Press, 2000), pp. 500–5.

85. Huntington, *Soldier and the State*, chaps. 2, 8–11, pp. 361–7; James L. Abrahamson, *America Arms for a New Century: The Making of a Great Military Power* (New York: Free Press, 1981), pp. 138–47; Karsten, *Naval Aristocracy*, 187–93.

86. In the TISS survey, the answers "agree strongly" or "agree somewhat" were given to the assertion, "The decline of traditional values is contributing to the breakdown of our society," according to the following distribution ("military" being defined as active-duty, reserve on active duty, and National Guard up-and-coming officers): military, 89 per cent; civilian elite, 70 percent; mass public, 82 percent. For the statement "Through leading by example, the military could help American society become more moral" the figures were military 70 percent and civilian elite 42 percent (the mass public was not surveyed on this question). For "Civilian society would be better off if it adopted more of the military's values and customs," the distribution was: military, 75 percent; civilian elite, 29 percent; and mass public, 37 percent. See also Davis, "Attitudes and Opinions," in *Soldiers and Civilians*, ed. Feaver and Kohn, pp. 116–9. For more analysis of the military view of civilian society, see Gronke and Feaver, "Uncertain Confidence," pp. 147ff. On p. 149 they write, "Elite military officers evaluate civilian society far more negatively than do elite civilians." The use of the military as a role model for society has a long history in American thinking; in the 1980s, the Chief of Naval Operations, James D. Watkins, was a leading proponent of that view. Peter Grier, "Navy as National Role Model?" *Christian Science Monitor*, 4 June 1986, p. 1.

87. Sam C. Sarkesian, "The U.S. Military Must Find Its Voice," *Orbis*, Summer 1998, pp. 423–37; James H. Webb, Jr., "The Silence of the Admirals," U.S. Naval Institute *Proceedings*, January 1999, pp. 29–34. Sarkesian expanded the argument in Sam C. Sarkesian and Robert E. Connor, Jr., *The U.S. Military Profession into the Twenty-first Century: War, Peace and Politics* (London: Frank Cass, 1999), esp. chaps. 11, 12. Even as respected and experienced a defense reporter as George C. Wilson has implied that the senior military leadership should speak out publicly in disagreement with their civilian superiors. This sentiment became something of a mantra in the middle and late 1990s as senior officers were accused of caving in to political correctness. See Wilson, "Joint Chiefs Need to Be More Gutsy," *National Journal*, 20 November 1999, p. 3418.

88. Webb, "Silence of the Admirals," p. 34.

89. Crowe, *Line of Fire*, p. 214. The 1998–99 TISS survey asked under what circumstances "it is acceptable for a military member to leak unclassified information or documents to the press." The figures for active-duty officers were (rounded up):

Opinion	Agree (%)	Disagree (%)	No Opinion (%)
"A crime has been committed and the chain of command is not acting on it."	26	70	4
"Doing so may prevent a policy that will lead to unnecessary casualties."	30	65	6
"Doing so discloses a course of action that is morally or ethically wrong."	28	65	7
"He or she is ordered to by a superior."	17	76	7
"Doing so brings to light a military policy or course of action that may lead to a disaster for the country."	39	55	6
"Never"	41	49	10

Reserve and National Guard officers were slightly more willing to agree to leak, but a higher percentage of them (46 percent) answered "never."

90. Peter J. Skibitski, "New Commandant Intends to Push for More Resources for Pentagon," *Inside the Navy*, 15 November 1999, p. 1; Hunter Keeter, "Marine Commandant Calls for Defense Spending Increase," *Defense Daily*, 16 August 2000, p. 6; John Robinson, "Outgoing 6th Fleet Commander Warns Fleet Size Is Too Small," *Defense Daily*, 22 September 2000, p. 1; Elaine M. Grossman, "Defense Budget Boost to 4 Percent of GDP Would Pose Dramatic Shift," *Inside the Pentagon*, 31 August 2000, p. 3; Steven Lee Myers, "A Call to Put the Budget Surplus to Use for the Military," *New York Times*, 28 September 2000, p. A24; Cindy Rupert, "Admiral: Navy Pales to Past One," *Tampa Tribune*, 21 October 2000, p. 2; Linda de France, "Senior Navy Officers: 'We Need More Ships, Planes, Subs,'" *Aerospace Daily*, 30 October 2000, and "In Next QDR, 'Budgets Need to Support Our Tasking,' General Says," *Aerospace Daily*, 4 December 2000; Vickii Howell, "Admiral Tells Civic Clubs Navy Needs More Ships, Subs," *Birmingham (Alabama) News*, 16 November 2000, p. 6B; Robert I. Natter, "Help Keep This the Greatest Navy," U.S. Naval Institute *Proceedings*, December 2000, p. 2; Rowan Scarborough, "Military Expects Bush to Perform," *Washington Times*, 26 December 2000, p. 1.

91. Rowan Scarborough, "Cohen Tells Military Leaders 'Not to Beat Drum with Tin Cup,'" *Washington Times*, 8 September 2000, p. 4. Secretary Cohen told them, according to his spokesman, "to be honest but. . . ." According to Thomas E. Ricks and Robert Suro, "Military Budget Maneuvers Target Next President," *Washington Post*, 5 June 2000, p. 1, the armed services began ignoring civilian orders on the budget as early as June 2000, in order to "target" the next administration. "'We're going for the big money,' an officer on the Joint Staff was quoted as saying. . . . Pentagon insiders say the Clinton administration, which long has felt vulnerable on military issues, doesn't believe it can afford a public feud with the chiefs—especially in the midst of Gore's campaign. So, these officials say, aides to defense Secretary William S. Cohen are seeking only to avoid confrontation and to tamp down the controversy. . . . One career bureaucrat in the Office of the Secretary of Defense said privately that he was offended by the arrogant tone service officials have used in recent discussions. . . . By contrast, a senior military official said the chiefs' budget demands represent a 'repudiation of bankrupt thinking' in both the White House and Congress, which have asked the military to conduct a growing number of missions around the world in recent years without paying the full bill."

92. Bradley Graham, "Joint Chiefs Doubted Air Strategy," *Washington Post*, 5 April 1999, p. A1. See also Kenneth R. Rizer [Maj., USAF], *Military Resistance to Humanitarian War in Kosovo and Beyond: An Ideological Explanation*, Air University Library, Fairchild Paper (Maxwell AFB, Ala.: Air Univ. Press, 2000), pp. 1–2, 7, 41–2.

93. The regular public promotion of service interests by officers began when the Navy and

Army in the late nineteenth and early twentieth centuries formed coherent understand-
ings of their own roles in national defense
and formal doctrines for war-fighting in their
respective domains of sea and land (and later
air). The institutionalization of service advice
on military subjects and public pronouncements on national security affairs has circum-
scribed civilian control to a degree. Efforts to
limit the military's public voice, beginning
perhaps in the first Wilson administration
(1913–17), have been episodic and often inef-
fective. See Allan R. Millett, *The American
Political System and Civilian Control of the
Military: A Historical Perspective* (Columbus:
Mershon Center of the Ohio State University,
1979), pp. 19, 27–30; Karsten, *Naval Aristocracy*, pp. 301–13, 362–71; Abrahamson,
America Arms for a New Century, pp. 147–50;
Betros, "Officer Professionalism," in press;
Johnson, *Fast Tanks and Heavy Bombers*,
pp. 68–9.

94. Published in New York by HarperCollins,
1997. The author was McMaster's adviser at
the University of North Carolina at Chapel
Hill, 1992–96, for the seminar papers, master's thesis, and Ph.D. dissertation that re-
sulted in the book.

95. McMaster hints at such an interpretation
only by implying that the Army chief of staff,
Harold K. Johnson, might have been justified
in resigning (p. 318); by implying that the
chiefs should have "confront[ed] the president with their objections to McNamara's approach to the war" (p. 328); by stating that
"the president . . . expected the Chiefs to lie"
and "the flag officers should not have toler-
ated it" (p. 331); and by blaming the chiefs
for going along with a strategy they believed
would fail, and thus sharing the culpability
with their deceitful civilian superiors for losing the war "in Washington, D.C., even before Americans assumed sole responsibility
for the fighting in 1965 and before they realized the country was at war; indeed, even before the first American units were deployed"
(pp. 333–4). The interpretation of long
standing in military thinking since the Vietnam War is that the war lacked clear objectives; that it was lost because a fallacious
strategy was imposed by deceitful politicians
who limited American power and
micromanaged military operations; and

because the American people, with no stake
in the war (in part because elites avoided service), were biased against the American effort
by a hostile press. Rosemary Mariner, a retired naval captain and pioneer naval aviator,
remembers "a certain litany to the Vietnam
War story" in "every ready room" and at every "happy hour" from "flight training and
throughout subsequent tactical aviation assignments" (she was commissioned in 1973),
a "tribal lore that Robert S. McNamara was
the devil incarnate whom the Joint Chiefs ob-
viously didn't have the balls to stand up to. . . .
Had the generals and admirals resigned in
protest or conducted some kind of a second
'admiral's revolt,' the war would have either
been won or stopped." Thus Mariner's "ini-
tial reaction to McMaster's book was that it
simply affirmed what had been viewed as
common wisdom." Conversation with the
author, 13 April 2000, Durham, N.C.; e-mail
to the author, 14 May 2001. Indications of
the impact of Vietnam on officer thinking are
in George C. Herring, "Preparing Not to
Fight the Last War: The Impact of the Vietnam War on the U.S. Military," in *After Vietnam: Legacies of a Lost War*, ed. Charles Neu
(Baltimore: Johns Hopkins Univ. Press,
2000), pp. 73–7; David Howell Petraeus, "The
American Military and the Lessons of Vietnam: A Study of Military Influence and the
Use of Force in the Post-Vietnam Era" (Ph.D.
dissertation, Princeton University, Princeton,
New Jersey, 1987); and Frank Hoffman, *Deci-
sive Force: The New American Way of War*
(Westport, Conn.: Praeger, 1996).

96. Fogleman explained his motives in a 1997 interview and specifically rejected the notion
that he resigned in protest. Kohn, ed., "Early
Retirement of Fogleman," pp. 6–23, esp. p. 20.

97. While there is no tradition of resignation in
the American armed forces, it has happened,
and occasionally senior officers have considered or threatened it. In 1907, "Admiral
Willard H. Brownson resigned as chief of
the Bureau of Navigation after the president
[Theodore Roosevelt], over Brownson's pro-
tests, appointed a surgeon rather than a line
officer to command a hospital ship." Oyos,
"Roosevelt, Congress, and the Military,"
p. 325. George C. Marshall offered or inti-
mated resignation, or was reported to have
done so, at least a half-dozen times when

chief of staff, but he claimed later to have actually threatened it only once—and in retrospect characterized his action as "reprehensible." Forrest C. Pogue, *George C. Marshall: Ordeal and Hope* (New York: Viking, 1966), pp. 461 n. 33, 97–103, 285–7, and *George C. Marshall: Organizer of Victory, 1943–1945* (New York: Viking, 1973), pp. 246–7, 492–3, 510–1. General Harold K. Johnson considered resigning several times, and in August 1967 the Joint Chiefs (absent one member) considered resigning as a group over the Vietnam War. See Lewis Sorley, *Honorable Warrior: General Harold K. Johnson and the Ethics of Command* (Lawrence: Univ. Press of Kansas, 1998), pp. 181–2, 223–4, 263, 268–70, 285–7, 303–4. In 1977, on a flight to Omaha from Washington, General F. Michael Rogers suggested to four of his colleagues that all of the Air Force's four-stars should resign over President Jimmy Carter's cancelation of the B-1 bomber, but nothing came of the discussion. See Erik Riker-Coleman, "Political Pressures on the Joint Chiefs of Staff: The Case of General David C. Jones," paper presented at the annual meeting of the Society for Military History, Calgary, Alberta, 27 May 2001. The source for the discussion of mass resignation is Bruce Holloway [Gen., USAF], oral history interview by Vaughn H. Gallacher [Lt. Col., USAF], 16–18 August 1977, pp. 424–6, U.S. Air Force Historical Research Agency, Maxwell AFB, Alabama. In a discussion about pressure to resign over the cancelation of the B-1, General David C. Jones (oral history interview by Lt. Col. Maurice N. Marynow, USAF, and Richard H. Kohn, August–October 1985 and January–March 1986, pp. 178–9, 181) commented, "I think there are cases where people should perhaps resign: first, if they are ever pressured to do something immoral, illegal, or unethical; second, if you possibly felt you hadn't had your day in court—if you hadn't been able to express your views; or if we had been inhibited in the conversation to the Congress. . . . It seems to me that it is very presumptuous that somebody in the military can set themselves up on a pedestal, that they have the answer to the country, that the President who has just been elected on a platform of cutting the defense budget, is somehow so

wrong that we are in this pedestal position, that we know the answers in this country. . . . It is up to the military to make its case, and then salute smartly once that case is made. . . . The only thing I have seen while I was in the military that really would be . . . a condition of resignation would be somehow during the Vietnam War. But probably . . . it would have been for the wrong reasons[—] . . . the White House . . . determining the targets . . . or whatever. The more fundamental reason is how in the world did we get ourselves involved in a land war in Southeast Asia[?] . . . [W]e are really servants of the people. The people make their decisions on the President. We are not elected; the President is elected. It's only in that regard if number one, they are trying to corrupt you by ignoring you and by muzzling you and all that sort of stuff. . . . Or if something is of such national importance, and I'm not sure anybody can predict it." In 1980, General Edward N. Meyer, chief of staff of the Army, was asked by the secretary of the Army to rescind a statement he had made to Congress about "a hollow army." Meyer refused and offered his resignation, but it was not accepted. Kitfield, *Prodigal Soldiers*, pp. 201–3. Retired Marine Corps commandant Charles C. Krulak (question and answer session, Joint Services Conference on Professional Ethics, Springfield, Virginia, 27–28 January 2000, enclosed in an e-mail from a colleague to the author, 1 February 2000) claimed that "it had become known within the Pentagon that 56 Marine General Officers would 'turn in their suits' if mixed gender training were imposed on the Marine Corps. . . . The Marines drew a line in the sand, and the opposition folded."

98. Colin L. Powell with Joseph E. Persico, *My American Journey* (New York: Random House, 1995), p. 167.

99. Ibid., p. 149. In May 1983, then Lieutenant Colonel Wesley Clark "suggested a line of argument" to then Brigadier General Powell for introducing a transition plan to the incoming Army chief of staff: "Isn't the most important thing never to commit U.S. troops again unless we're going in to win? No more gradualism and holding back like in Vietnam, but go in with overwhelming force?" According to Clark, "Powell agreed. . . .

This argument captured what so many of us felt after Vietnam." Clark, *Waging Modern War*, p. 7. Clark remembered that "in the Army, it had long been an article of resolve that there would be 'no more Vietnams,' wars in which soldiers carried the weight of the nation's war despite the lack of public support at home" (p. 17).

100. Ole R. Holsti, "Of Chasms and Convergences: Attitudes and Beliefs of Civilians and Military Elites at the Start of a New Millennium," in *Soldiers and Civilians*, ed. Feaver and Kohn, pp. 84, 489, and tables 1.27, 1.28.

101. Ronald T. Kadish [Lt. Gen., USAF], Director, Ballistic Missile Defense Organization, "Remarks," 6 December 2000, Space and Missile Defense Symposium and Exhibition, Association of the United States Army, El Paso, Texas, on the World Wide Web at http://www.ausa.org/kadish.html (5 January 2000).

102. Frank Hoffman e-mail to the author, 14 March 2000. Hoffman, a member of the national security study group assisting the U.S. Commission on National Security/21st Century, reported his conversation with a "Joint Staff Officer that the Joint Staff and the military officers in the NSC were coordinating a rapid schedule to preclude the president from announcing a Clinton Doctrine on the use of force in late October. It was expressed in the conversation that it was hoped that publishing a strategy with narrow use of force criteria would cut out the president from contradicting himself late in the month in a speech that would contravene the military's idea of how to use military force."

103. Kohn, ed., "Early Retirement of Fogleman," p. 12.

104. "Why is it . . . that whatever the question is—enforcing a peace agreement in Bosnia, evacuating the U.N. from Bosnia, or invading Haiti, the answer is always 25,000 Army troops?" asked one Marine officer of a reporter. By mid-1995, the uniformed leadership was more divided on opposing interventions. See Thomas E. Ricks, "Colin Powell's Doctrine on Use of Military Force Is Now Being Questioned by Senior U.S. Officers," *Wall Street Journal*, 30 August 1995, p. A12; Quinn-Judge, "Doubts of Top Brass," p. 12.

105. Kohn, ed., "Early Retirement of Fogleman," p. 18. Another possible resignation was voiced privately in 2000. Conversation with a senior military officer, January 2001.

106. In "The Pentagon, Not Congress or the President, Calls the Shots," *International Herald Tribune*, 6 August 2001, on the World Wide Web at http://www.iht.com/articles/28442.htm (5 December 2001), journalist William Pfaff calls the military "the most powerful institution in American government, in practice largely unaccountable to the executive branch." He considers the Pentagon's "power in Congress" to be "unassailable." In "The Praetorian Guard," *National Interest*, Winter 2000/2001, pp. 57–64, Pfaff asserts (p. 63) that American "military forces play a larger role in national life than their counterparts in any state outside the Third World." See also Desch, *Civilian Control*, chap. 3 and appendix; Charles Lane, "TRB from Washington," *New Republic*, 15 November 1999, p. 8; Melvin Goodman, "Shotgun Diplomacy: The Dangers of Letting the Military Control Foreign Policy," *Washington Monthly*, December 2000, pp. 46–51; Gore Vidal, "Washington, We Have a Problem," *Vanity Fair*, December 2000, pp. 136ff.

107. For the long-term congressional forfeiture of authority in national security, see Louis Fisher, *Congressional Abdication on War & Spending* (College Station: Texas A&M Univ. Press, 2000), chaps. 1–4.

108. The oath every American military officer takes upon commissioning reads: "I, [name], do solemnly swear (or affirm) that I will support and defend the Constitution of the United States against all enemies, foreign and domestic; that I will bear true faith and allegiance to the same; that I take this obligation freely, without any mental reservation or purpose of evasion; and that I will well and faithfully discharge the duties of the office on which I am about to enter. So help me God." The requirement and wording is in 5 U.S.C. §3331 (1966). An oath to support the Constitution is required of "all executive and judicial officers" as well as senators and representatives, of the national and state governments, by Article VI, para. 3.

109. For civilian control in the Constitution, see Richard H. Kohn, "The Constitution and

National Security: The Intent of the Framers," in *The United States Military under the Constitution of the United States, 1789-1989*, ed. Richard H. Kohn (New York: New York Univ. Press, 1991), pp. 61–94.

110. This is George Bush's characterization, in "A Nation Blessed," *Naval War College Review*, Autumn 2001, p. 138. The actual civil-military relationship and the extent of civilian oversight are revealed in the works cited in endnote 111, below.

111. A good bibliography of the literature on the Vietnam War is George C. Herring, *America's Longest War: The United States and Vietnam, 1950–1975*, 3d ed. (New York: McGraw-Hill, 1996). The most convincing explanations of the American defeat explore the inability of the United States and South Vietnam to prevent communist forces from contesting the countryside and thereby continuing combat, and the failure to establish an indigenous government that could command the loyalty or obedience of the population, in the crucial period 1965–68, before the American people lost patience with the cost and inconclusiveness of the struggle and forced American disengagement. The best discussion to date of civil-military relations in the Persian Gulf War is Michael R. Gordon and General Bernard E. Trainor, *The Generals' War: The Inside Story of the Conflict in the Gulf* (Boston: Little, Brown, 1995). The memoirs of Generals Powell and Schwarzkopf confirm the very strong oversight and occasional intervention by the Bush administration in strategy and operations during the fighting. The senior British commander in the Gulf, General Sir Peter de la Billiere, *Storm Command: A Personal Account* (London: HarperCollins, 1992), remembers (p. 103) that "Schwarzkopf was under intense pressure from Washington . . . to consider other plans being dreamt up by amateur strategists in the Pentagon," but (pp. 139–40) that as late as early December 1990 he "had no written directive as to how he should proceed[,] . . . no precise instructions as to whether he was to attack Iraq as a whole, march on Baghdad, capture Saddam, or what." See also George Bush and Brent Scowcroft, *A World Transformed* (New York: Random House, 1998), pp. 302ff.

112. That civilian control includes the right of the civilians to be "wrong" is the insight of Peter D. Feaver. See his "The Civil-Military Problematique: Huntington, Janowitz and the Question of Civilian Control," *Armed Forces & Society*, vol. 23, 1996, p. 154.

113. The importance of firm civilian control, even to the point of interference in technical military matters, in order to assure a strong connection between ends and means, is the argument of Eliot A. Cohen, "The Unequal Dialogue," in *Soldiers and Civilians*, ed. Feaver and Kohn, chap. 12.

114. S. L. A. Marshall, the famous journalist and reserve officer who from the 1930s through the 1970s studied and wrote so influentially about soldiers, soldiering, battle, and war, was not contrasting the military from other professions but people in uniform from all others when he wrote: "The placing of the line of duty above the line of self interest . . . is all that distinguishes the soldier from the civilian. And if that aspect of military education is slighted for any reason, the nation has lost its main hold on security." *The Soldier's Load and the Mobility of a Nation* (1947; repr. Quantico, Va.: Marine Corps Association, 1980), p. 104.

115. I am indebted to University of North Carolina at Chapel Hill emeritus professor of political science Raymond Dawson for this distinction.

116. Since the end of the Cold War, the Department of Defense has created at least three new institutes for security studies to teach democratic defense practices, particularly civilian control of the military, to other nations. Presently there are at least four, meant to serve uniformed officers, defense officials, and political leaders from formerly communist countries in Europe and Central Asia, Latin America, Africa, and the Asia-Pacific region.

117. Larry Rohter, "Fear of Loss of Democracy Led Neighbors to Aid Return," *New York Times*, 15 April 2002, p. A6; Christopher Marquis, "Bush Officials Met with Venezuelans Who Ousted Leader," *New York Times*, 16 April 2002, pp. A1, A8; and Peter Hakim, "Democracy and U.S. Credibility," *New York Times*, 21 April 2002, p. 4 wk.

118. Speech to the House of Commons, 11 November 1947, quoted in Robert Rhodes James, ed., *Winston S. Churchill: His Complete Speeches*, 8 vols. (New York: Chelsea House, 1974), vol. 7, p. 7566.

CPSIA information can be obtained
at www.ICGtesting.com
Printed in the USA
LVHW04s0011310818
588760LV00003B/72/P